STAGE SOUND

STAGE SOUND

David Collison

Foreword by Peter Hall

STUDIO VISTA

To Annie. Met in Chapter 1 – married in
Chapter 7. And an awful lot of typing . . .

A Studio Vista book published by
Cassell & Collier Macmillan Publishers Ltd,
35 Red Lion Square, London WC1R 4SG
and at Sydney, Auckland, Toronto, Johannesburg
an affiliate of
Macmillan Publishing Co., Inc.,
New York

ISBN 0 289 70570 3

Set in Univers 9 on 10 point
Printed in Great Britain by
Fletcher & Son Ltd, Norwich

ACKNOWLEDGEMENTS

There are many people who have been kind
enough to lend their assistance in the prepa-
ration of this book. I should particularly like to
thank John Pilcher not only for his interest but
also for the many hours spent on the technical
drawings. It is difficult to know how to express
my gratitude to Robert ('you-can't-say-that')
Higham who with tremendous patience, verg-
ing on enthusiasm, vetted the technical sections of the book.

I am indebted to BASF United Kingdom
Limited for permission to draw liberally from
their booklet on tape recording. And I am similarly obliged to AKG Equipment Limited for
allowing me to include sections from their
booklet on microphones. I am grateful to
Blandford Press for allowing me to use items
from *Hi-fi in the Home* in the glossary.

I have to thank Peter Hall as the director who
first inspired and encouraged me in my chosen
profession and, later, Michael Elliott who has
the foresight to allow his creative technical
team the freedom of experimentation. I was
very lucky to meet and team up with lighting
designer and founder of Theatre Projects Ltd
Richard Pilbrow during one of Michael
Elliott's productions. And in 1962 on the Lionel
Bart musical *Blitz* I was fortunate enough to
meet Antony Horder who has been my close
friend and colleague ever since.

Finally, I feel I must mention three great
innovators. Men who started the first three
firms specializing in electronically reproduced
sound for the British theatre. I am proud to be
able to say that I knew, and learned a great deal
from all three: Jack Bishop, R. G. Jones and
Bill Walton – the theatre is in their debt.

Contents

Foreword

As a young director, I filled my plays with sounds. They not only gave atmosphere; at dramatic moments, their sudden absence made silence even more telling.

So I went to enormous pains to create a world of sound for each play. I think that the actors, once they were over the first moments of the dress rehearsal where it appeared that they had to share their lines with rampant bullfrogs and incessant crickets, were supported and helped by the sounds around them.

All the same, I hadn't yet learned that all effects in the theatre which are nice but are not absolutely necessary should be cut. I think I quickly understood one thing: atmospheric sound in the theatre must be so faint as to be almost indiscernible. Noticeable sounds can only be supported by noticeable (and essential) actions. The amount of sound, evident or subliminal, depends of course on the play. Shakespeare does not need perpetual soundtracks; but the poetic realism of Tenessee Williams does.

I was fortunate twenty-one years ago, in those early experiments in sound, to encounter a technician of genius: David Collison. He could cue a sound to a tenth of a second — by hand on a pick-up. We didn't use tape then. Surrounded by three or four turntables and a mass of records, he built up a soundtrack which was at one with the dialogue. He would have made one of the great Dubbing Mixers (the man who balances all the various sounds in the final stages of a film) of all time.

Fortunately, he stayed in the theatre. His work with Theatre Projects has provided excellent sound facilities for every kind of theatre. And although he has for many years been able to do the impossible with sound, he has the humility of every great theatre technician. He knows that sounds, lights, and elaborate stage effects are nothing if the words are not just, and the actor expressing them true.

This book is like the man: modest, precise, and unexpectedly humorous. I believe it will prove invaluable.

PETER HALL
11 June 1975

Introduction

The aim of this book is to assist (and, I hope, inspire) the non-technical user of sound equipment whether for a play or musical, a fashion show or an after dinner speech.

The first section is devoted to an explanation of basic electronic and acoustic facts which can directly affect the handling of sound equipment. Although this information will be elementary to some readers it can still serve as a useful reference. Others will find it a great help in fully appreciating the later chapters.

The second half of the book discusses aspects of the practical handling of sound equipment, the creation of sound effects (both live and recorded) and the application of different types of loudspeakers and microphones under various conditions. Techniques and problems are highlighted by many examples taken from my own experience.

I was very pleased, though somewhat daunted, to be asked to write this book not only because of the honour it afforded but because I was becoming increasingly aware of the lack of any publication covering this particular field. This, however, is not altogether surprising. Electronically reproduced sound has only in the 1970s reached a sufficiently high standard in the theatre to be generally accepted as a technical art. Before then it suffered from a lack of interest caused largely by an ignorance of its potential, and a resultant lack of money. For these reasons the equipment was often not of the best quality and the person handling it not the most experienced.

As far back as the thirties, lighting designers began to use remote control switchboards and in the sixties miniaturization and duplicate 'preset' switchboards came in with the development of the thyristor dimmer. It was all becoming very sophisticated. Even scenery began to be more motorized and mechanized, while sound remained very much the poor relation. Audio engineers in other spheres such as radio, films and recording studios would scoff at the efforts of the few enthusiasts who were striving

for better standards in the theatre. It was not until 1973 that I actually met a television sound engineer who, at a recording of a theatre show, asked if he could take a direct feed from the theatre system. Acceptance at last.

In the days before microphones, gramophone records and tape recorders, sound in the theatre depended on mechanical and live effects. The creation of these was a great art and was usually the domain of the property department. Thunder storms, avalanches, railway trains and collapsing buildings, all could be created by a team of well rehearsed stage hands. I believe that as late as the 1940s the great Sir Donald Wolfit, for his storm scene in *King Lear*, had a carefully worked out sequence using the constant backing of a mechanical wind machine varying in speed and pitch as required plus, on cue, one person rattling a metal thunder sheet, another performing rumblings and crashes on a large bass thunder drum, while a fourth person was actually inside an enormous galvanized tank savagely belabouring the sides with two padded drumsticks. (It is said that Sir Donald could make himself heard above the lot and while doing so was able to detect if any one of the 'elements' was not performing strictly as rehearsed.)

When I began stage managing in the mid-fifties, although gramophone records had very much taken over, stage management still often preferred to do certain effects live. And managements, rather than hire expensive sound equipment and records, would insist, say, that a mechanical wind or wave machine be used. Extremely effective they could be too.

If recorded effects were required the stage manager would go with his shopping list to one of the theatre sound companies and purchase discs of the fairly limited range of stock items. He would then arrange the hire of some equipment which would duly be delivered and installed in the theatre. After that it was up to the stage management and the director to get on with it. It was simply unfortunate if the loudspeakers were the wrong type, if there was insufficient power to achieve the required effect, or if nobody knew about loudspeaker placing or the sound absorbent properties of various scenic materials, etc.

I was fortunate enough at that time to be working with some directors who liked using sound. And as I very much enjoyed operating sound equipment I found myself becoming a specialist. This was at the beginning of the tape revolution which took place in the British theatre during the late fifties and early sixties. The 'quality' revolution really got under way in the seventies and is still continuing.

Microphones for speech reinforcement were used in the forties and fifties. But the systems remained pretty crude until the late sixties when certain composers, used to having complete control over a sound balance inside a recording studio, began to write material for the stage which necessitated similar techniques. Producers were forced to pay for it and a new range of theatre sound equipment emerged. The rock movement, from the Beatles onwards, also helped, because people began to accept electronic sound. Prior to this period of change the poor stage manager had once again to assess the microphone requirements and organize the rental of what he deemed to be suitable equipment. This usually consisted of microphones on raised stands along the front of the stage, a set of two or four column loudspeakers driven by one or two amplifiers and a simple mixer with an overall master and tone controls. Once installed the usual procedure was: turn the master knob up for songs and down for dialogue. This is a far cry from the sophisticated mixing desks that are now installed in theatres where the balance engineer individually controls sometimes thirty or more microphones.

However, it is early days. For although the sound man is now an accepted member of the theatrical creative team there is still much to do to improve the equipment and the techniques. Hopefully, this book may help somebody along that road.

PART 1

1 What is sound?

PRESSURE WAVES

Sound is essentially the movement of air in the form of pressure waves radiating from the source at a speed of about 1,130 feet (350 metres) per second. These waves consist of alternate regions of high and low pressure travelling *in all directions* like a continually expanding sphere. Sound cannot travel in a vacuum because a medium is required on which the pressure waves can act and all solids, liquids and gases will transmit sound to a greater or lesser degree.

In order to understand the behaviour of sound waves a useful analogy may be drawn from a study of the ripples that are set up when a small stone is dropped into a pond (remembering that water ripples move in one plane only and sound waves expand in all directions). Small waves travel outwards, gradually diminishing in height; in sound terms, diminishing in intensity or loudness. However, although the ripples get smaller the distance between adjacent peaks, the wavelength, is constant. One cycle of vibration occurs when the water

surface at a given point changes from peak to trough and back to peak again, i.e. a complete cycle of events.

FREQUENCY

If the stone were attached to a piece of string, it would be possible to vibrate it up and down at the surface of the water. If this could be done one hundred times each second, one hundred waves would be created each second and there would be one hundred cycles of vibration each second at a point on the water surface, (see point A in fig. 1). Thus the frequency of the vibration would be 100 cycles per second, and the unit used for measuring cycles per second is Hertz (Hz). The rate of vibration is the frequency or pitch of the sound and so the higher the rate at which waves pass a given point, the higher is the pitch of the sound. An oscilloscope is a device for displaying visually an electronic signal. It is used for accurately studying the characteristics of a signal. Figs 2, 3, 4 and 5 show oscilloscopes displaying different frequencies.

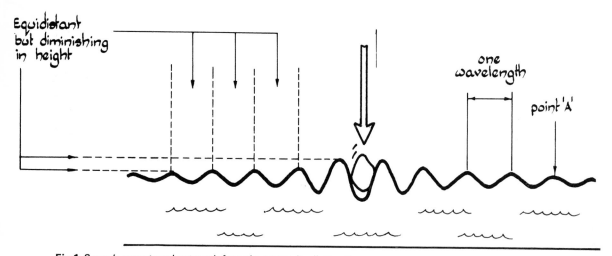

Fig 1 *Sound waves travel outwards from the source in all directions.*

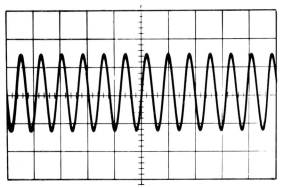

Fig 2 *Oscilloscope displaying a pure high frequency tone.*

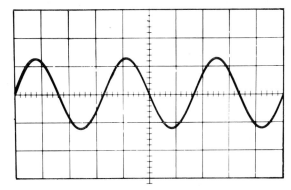

Fig 3 *Oscilloscope displaying a pure low frequency tone (fewer waves – or cycles – per second).*

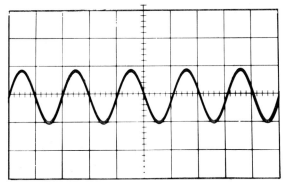

Fig 4 *Oscilloscope displaying a pure tone at a given intensity.*

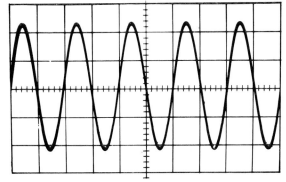

Fig 5 *Oscilloscope displaying the same tone at increased intensity.*

INTENSITY

To obtain a greater intensity of sound at the same pitch we require the same number of cycles per second, but the movement between peak and trough must be greater. Returning to the water analogy, if a larger stone had been vibrated 100 times every second, 100 larger waves would have been produced. The greater the size or amplitude of the pressure waves, the greater the intensity or loudness of the sound.

The human ear is capable of hearing sounds with a very wide range of intensities. In terms of air pressure changes, the loudest sound which does not quite cause physical pain is about one million times greater than the quietest sound which the ear can just detect. Because such large numbers are inconvenient to handle, sound intensities are often referred to in terms of decibels (dB). Strictly, the decibel refers to the ratio of two intensities or amplitudes, and it is calculated logarithmically. By this means we achieve a convenient unit in which one decibel represents about the smallest change in sound intensity which the human ear can detect.

The difference in intensity between the sound of leaves rustling gently and a symphony orchestra at its loudest is about 100 dB. If we set our standard level of 0dB intensity at the sound of rustling leaves, the orchestra will be +100 dB of sound. Alternatively, if we set our 0 dB for the orchestra, the sound of rustling leaves will then be −100 dB. Fig. 6 shows the intensities for various sounds.

Sound levels are subjective, however, and the ear quickly adjusts to growing intensities. Not until the sound equipment is being overloaded are some people convinced of the loudness.

DOPPLER EFFECT

It is interesting to note that an approaching sound, say of a police siren, appears to be higher pitched than a receding sound. This is because as the source approaches you are receiving more cycles each second than when it is going away from you. This phenomenon is called the Doppler effect after an Austrian, Christian Johann Doppler (1803–53), who first explained it.

HARMONICS

Pure sounds (i.e. single undistorted frequencies) occur very rarely in nature and are produced mainly by electronic apparatus especially designed for the purpose. A variable frequency oscillator is one such piece of equipment used by engineers to test other electronic equipment. It produces the pure waves as depicted above on the oscilloscope. Electronic organs and synthesizers are based on the oscillator with distortion deliberately introduced to vary the quality of the sound.

Most sounds consist of a complex mixture of frequencies at differing intensities.

Sounds produced by musical instruments usually consist of the basic note or fundamental and small amounts of integral multiples of this frequency or harmonics (in musical terms, overtones). Thus a piano note of fundamental frequency 200 Hz will contain proportions of 400 Hz, of 600 Hz, of 800 Hz, etc. No two instruments will produce exactly the same proportion of harmonics and it is this varying characteristic which determines the *timbre* of each instrument.

In most musical instruments, sound is produced by causing part of them to vibrate. When the bow is drawn across a violin string, this vibration imparts energy through the bridge to the body of the violin which tries to follow the vibration. In so striving the wood produces pressure waves which, though not the same, are nevertheless related to the fundamental vibrations of the string, i.e. harmonics. We therefore have a combination of frequencies which are characteristic of the violin. Similar examples are the vibrations of reeds in woodwind instruments and the shock waves of drum skins or cymbals when struck. Trumpet and horn players cause their own lips to vibrate in the mouthpiece of their instrument.

THE EAR

We shall see in later chapters how the tiny movements of the diaphragm of a microphone when struck by sound waves set up electrical vibrations or impulses. These impulses in turn may be electronically amplified and made to cause a loudspeaker to vibrate similarly, setting up pressure waves and thereby reproducing the sound.

Sound waves cause the ear drum to vibrate just like the diaphragm of a microphone. These tiny movements are transmitted to the base of the cochlea which contains an incompressible fluid. The fluid transmits the vibrations equally to all surfaces of the cochlea where numerous nerve endings react and transmit auditory sensations to the brain.

The average human ear can hear sounds from 16 Hz to 16,000 Hz, although some people can hear as high as 23,000 Hz. Frequencies below the lowest which can normally be heard are called infrasonic and those above the highest are called ultrasonic. Sensitivity to higher frequencies deteriorates with age so that, typically, someone in their sixties does not hear anything above 6,000 Hz. The human voice ranges from 40–1200 Hz, and a piano ranges from 30–4,000 Hz. See fig. 8 for further comparisons.

Although the ear transmits to the brain all the sounds it manages to collect we are able, to an amazing degree, to select what we want to hear. (Just pause for a moment and listen to the sounds that are going on around you. Many of them will have been subconsciously blocked out.) We can be selective in another way when listening to complex sounds; it is possible, for example, to identify the different instruments playing in a full orchestra and even to 'tune in' to one in particular.

The human ear collects sounds forwards and sideways and can determine the source of sounds within approximately 15 degrees horizontally. Because the ears are positioned on the sides of the head we find it more difficult to

Sound Pressure Levels
(i.e. dB ref. 0.0002 µbar)

THRESHOLD OF PAIN	140	Jet aircraft at 15 feet
		Artillery fire
THRESHOLD OF FEELING	120	Underground train
		Noisy industrial plant
	100	Large symphony orchestra (forte)
		Listening level of a Hi-Fi addict!
	80	Inside a family car
		Noisy office
ENVELOPE OF HEARING	60	Conversation
		Suburban street
	40	Quiet home
		Bedroom
		Quiet whisper
	20	Empty theatre
		Rustling leaves
THRESHOLD OF AUDIBILITY	0	Inside a heavily treated room (e.g. Recording Studio)

Fig 6 *Chart showing typical sound pressure levels measured in dB where OdB is defined as the threshold of audibility.*

13

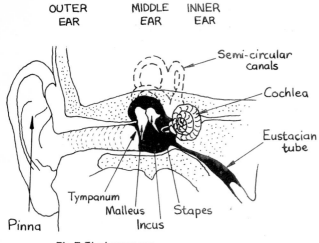

OUTER EAR   MIDDLE EAR   INNER EAR

Fig 7 *The human ear*

Functions

Pinna : *collects sound waves*

Tympanum *(ear drum)* : *vibrates by sound waves (like a microphone diaphragm)*

Ear Ossicles *(malleus – hammer, incus – anvil, stapes – stirrup): tiny bones which pick up and intensify vibrations*

Cochlea : *contains sensitive nerve endings which convert vibrations into nervous impulses to pass along the auditory nerve to the brain*

Eustachian tube : *carries air, keeping pressure in middle ear constant with outer atmosphere*

Semi-circular canals : *three tubes at right angles contain sensitive nerve endings affected by the fluid in the canals as the body moves. Important in balancing the body*

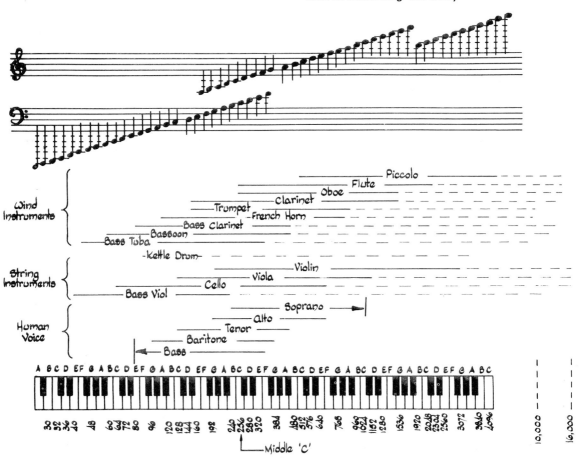

Fig 8 *Useful frequency comparisons*

determine the source of sounds vertically. This deficiency should be borne in mind when placing loudspeakers on a stage.

REVERBERATION (Multiple echoes)

Sound which is reflected several times between the surfaces of an enclosed space before reaching the ear is known as reverberation, and the reverberation time is the time taken for the sound intensity to drop to one millionth of its original intensity (by 60 dB) after the sound source has stopped. If the reverberation time in a theatre is greater than about $1\frac{1}{2}$ seconds, then direct speech tends to overlap and intelligibility is impaired.

Sounds emanating from above or behind a listener arrive after being reflected at various surfaces like walls, floor, ceiling, etc. Depending upon their acoustic properties, these sur-faces will alter the sound by absorbing certain frequencies and accentuating others. Basically, soft surfaces (drapes, clothes) absorb sound and hard surfaces reflect it. Since the reverberation may be greater in square or rectangular halls, theatres are usually designed to avoid parallel walls.

There is less reverberation at the higher frequencies (which give intelligibility to speech and 'brilliance' to music) because they are generally more easily absorbed. Therefore in practical terms high frequencies can be looked upon as directional.

It is generally known that as the intensity of a sound is increased the resulting audible reverberation will be proportionately longer. This fact can be used to advantage for sound effects. For example, if a recording of a gunshot is played in an auditorium and then, without changing the intensity, it is repeated with some artificial reverberation added (see Chapter 7) the effect will be of a louder sound.

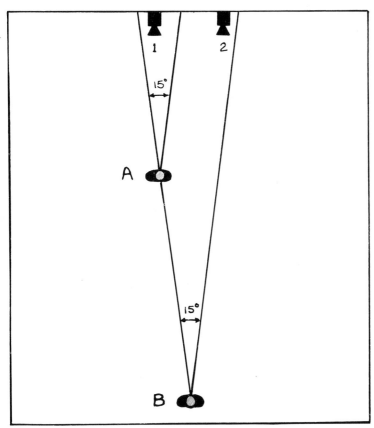

Fig 9 *Listener A can easily pinpoint the locations of loudspeakers 1 and 2, but listener B cannot tell the difference.*

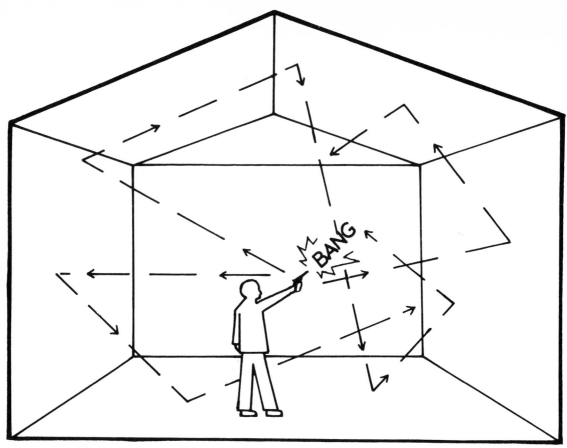

Fig 10 *Sound reflects off all hard surfaces and will carry on reflecting until it is eventually absorbed.*

2 Basic equipment

Having discussed some of the properties of sound, we shall now consider how to capture, amplify and reproduce it. For this certain basic items of equipment are required, which, leaving aside the process of recording which will be dealt with in a later chapter, fall roughly into five categories.

1 *Units which transmit a signal* such as microphones, tape and disc reproducers. We can also include radio tuners, electric guitars, synthesizers and a host of electronic devices which have one thing in common: they require amplification.

2 *Preamplifiers* These are usually built in to the mixer, amplifier, tape recorder, etc, in order to amplify incoming signals to a standard level. If this is done it is much more convenient to handle the signal through such devices as filters, bass, treble, presence and volume controls which we shall meet later.

3 *Mixers* These are used for combining a number of signals. Each input on the mixer has a volume control which varies the amount of the input signal to be mixed into the final output.

4 *Amplifiers* The final blended signal from the mixer is fed to an amplifier which magnifies that signal to a level at which a loudspeaker will respond.

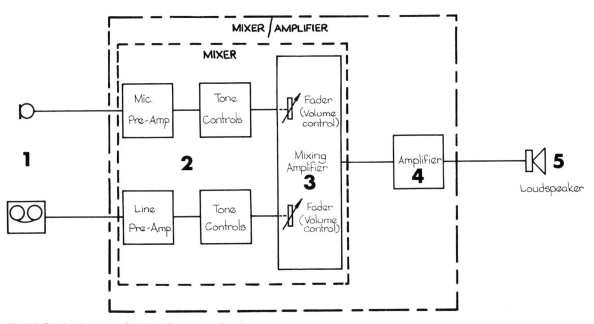

Fig 11 *The basic system falls into five categories: 1 units which transmit a signal 2 preamplifiers 3 mixers 4 amplifiers 5 loudspeakers*

5 *Loudspeakers* These translate the electrical vibrations from the amplifier back into pressure waves, i.e. sound, and the cycle is complete. Headphones also come into this category although most headsets are sensitive enough to operate from the preamplifier or mixing stage.

A simple example of the use of this basic equipment is the small public address system which might be used for garden fêtes or in church halls. This consists of a microphone, an amplifier, incorporating a preamplifier with a gain control determining the amount of signal from the microphone that will reach the amplifier, tone controls, adjusting the amount of treble and bass response, and a loudspeaker (photograph 1).

Photograph 2 shows a more complex sound system designed for theatre touring purposes, which is, however, based on exactly the same principles. Here a tape machine and microphones feed into the console which has a mixer with individual gain controls for each sound source, plus master controls and tone controls for the amplifiers, and speaker switching for selecting one or a number of loudspeakers.

A recording studio again uses the same principle. The microphones in the studio are connected to the mixing desk which in turn feeds amplifiers and monitor loudspeakers. The only difference is that the mixing desk not only feeds the amplifiers and monitor loudspeakers, it also feeds a tape recorder. This tape recorder can itself become a source when the playback from the tape recorder is connected back into the desk for purposes of listening to the recording later.

All sound systems, including the complex installation in the National Theatre of Great Britain which is described in the last chapter, are broadly based on this principle: sources – preamplifiers – mixer – amplifiers – loudspeakers.

INPUTS AND OUTPUTS

Because of the varying standards of connections in sound equipment, one has to use units which are designed to be connected together.

We must ascertain the following information about the inputs and outputs of the equipment: whether it is microphone level or line level, high impedance or low impedance, balanced or unbalanced. There is a further complication with the connection of amplifiers to loudspeakers, since loudspeakers can either be fed at low voltage or at high voltage.

To understand what is meant when we talk about inputs and outputs, it is necessary to know a little about voltages and impedance. Let us look for a moment at another water analogy, this time with reference to electricity. Imagine water flowing through a pipe:

1 The pressure of water = voltage – volts
2 Restriction of water flow in the pipe, i.e. smallness of bore = resistance – ohms or impedance
3 The rate of flow = current – amps

IMPEDANCE

Impedance is similar to resistance but the term impedance is reserved for use with alternating current (AC). For limiting the amount of current passing a given point, we can use resistors, inductors and capacitors (condensers). The unit of resistance used when measuring the resistance of resistors and the impedance of inductors and capacitors is called an ohm.

Inductors and capacitors have another very important property in electronic circuits in that they have different effects on low and high frequencies. A simple tone control could consist of a selection of capacitors connected across the signal wires. Depending upon which capacitor is chosen more or less of the high frequencies would be shorted out relative to the low frequencies.

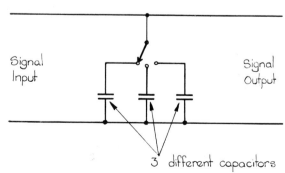

Fig 12 *A simple tone control. Selecting one or other of the different capacitors will short out more or less of, say, the high frequencies relative to the low.*

SIGNAL LEVELS

The input and output levels of equipment are given by the manufacturer either in volts or millivolts (mV) (a millivolt is one thousandth of a volt) or in decibels (dB). We met the decibel earlier as a ratio of sound intensities; it appears again as a ratio of voltages.

So that everybody knows what they are talking about, a standard reference level has been set in which 0 dB is equivalent to 0·775 volts.

The British GPO, who regulate such standards in the UK, chose this voltage many years ago because it gave the required power into their 600 ohms cables. Although 0·775 volts is rather an odd value it does not really matter because it is seldom necessary to convert backwards and forwards.

CONVERSION TABLE

Decibels	Voltages
+20 dB	7·75 V
+2·2 dB	1 V
0 dB	0·775 V
−17·8 dB	100 mV
−20 dB	77·5 mV
−37·8 dB	10 mV
−40 dB	7·75 mV
−57·8 dB	1 mV
−60 dB	0·775 mV
−80 dB	0·0775 mV

i.e. each time the decibels drop by 20 the voltage is divided by 10.

The voltages usually found between microphones, preamplifiers, mixers and amplifiers range between −80 dB and +10 dB, i.e. between about 1 millivolt and 3 volts. These are quite small voltages when compared with mains of 250 volts. Even the signal from an amplifier to its loudspeaker only reaches 40 volts for a 16 ohm loudspeaker delivering 100 watts. Incidentally, this power is usually regarded as too much for domestic use although it is quite acceptable in a large auditorium.

It is here that we have one of the main compromises in handling sound. If the signal voltage is too small it is very susceptible to interference or noise (hum, clicks, hiss, etc.), and special precautions have to be taken against this by using expensive screened cables and boxes to house the equipment. Conversely, if a large signal voltage is chosen it is difficult to achieve this level without distortion and the amplifiers become inconveniently large and heavy. So a compromise is made where the signal levels between preamplifiers, mixers and amplifiers is about 1 volt or 0 dB (zero level).

Signal levels of sound systems are divided broadly into two categories: microphone levels and line levels.

MICROPHONE LEVELS

Microphones generate small voltages from about −80 dB up to about −20 dB, depending on the loudness of the sound, and the method used in the microphone to convert from sound to electricity. There are two main categories, however.

1 *Low impedance microphones* These are in the range 30 and 600 ohms. Professional ribbon microphones are usually 30–50 ohms. Professional dynamic and condenser microphones are usually 200 or 300 ohms.

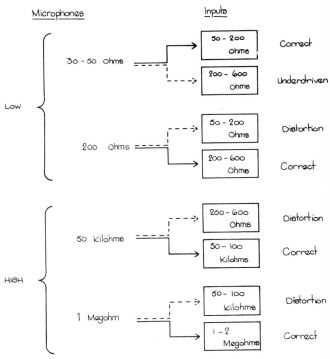

Fig 13 *A guide to suitable inputs for various microphone impedances*

2 *High impedance microphones* These are mainly the cheaper domestic variety. Many are dynamic microphones of 50,000 ohms (50K ohms). The really high impedance units, e.g. very cheap crystal microphones, are of two million ohms (two megohms).

Microphone inputs to amplifiers are stated by the manufacturer and will be as follows: (*a*) 'Low' – 30 to 50 ohms or 200 to 600 ohms (*b*) 'High' – or greater than 50,000 ohms and often as high as 2 megohms.

It is worth noting that satisfactory results may be obtained if a microphone is used with an input of higher impedance, for example a 30 ohm microphone with a 300 ohm input, but the amplification will be less than it would be with the correct input. The reverse, however, is not true. If a high impedance microphone is used with a 'low' input, serious distortion and loss of bass frequency will result. This is summarized in fig. 13.

LINE LEVELS

Usually the voltages of line level outputs (i.e. the pre-amp stages of tape recorders, mixers, etc.) are greater than those of microphones, and range from about −20 dB up to 0 dB (*zero level*).

The impedances usually found at line inputs and line outputs vary widely even in professional equipment. The original standard was that a line output was 600 ohms and this could be connected to the 600 ohm line input of the next piece of equipment in the chain. In this way the two items of equipment were said to be matched. However, this arrangement is operationally inflexible because, although one microphone should never be connected to more than one microphone input of an amplifier, it is often necessary to connect the line output of a mixer to the line inputs of several loudspeaker amplifiers. The technique used today is to keep the line output (usually) well below 600 ohms, typically 50 to 100 ohms, and the line input never less than 2,000 ohms and usually about 10,000 ohms.

Returning to our water analogy, we see that a high resistance can be likened to small-bore pipe and a low resistance to a large diameter pipe. It is obvious that a large pipe can supply water to many other pipes of small-bore with-

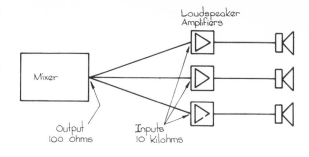

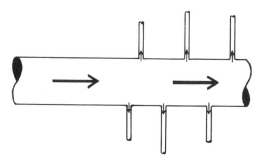

Fig 14 *Low impedance at line level can feed into high impedance just as a large bore water pipe can feed many small bore pipes. The addition or subtraction of a single small bore pipe will not noticeably affect the main flow (or signal).*

out difficulty and that adding a further small-bore pipe will not appreciably affect the flow in all the others. This is the principle of 'low into high' where one low impedance output can be connected to several high impedance inputs. Further high impedance inputs can be added without affecting the existing signal levels. There is obviously some limitation to the total number of inputs which can be connected to one output and with typical values of 100 ohms for the line output and 10,000 ohms for the line input it would usually be quite satisfactory to connect up to ten. High impedance inputs such as these are also known as bridging inputs.

The 'low into high' arrangement is highly recommended for professional and semi-professional installations where flexibility is important.

Caution This technique only applies at line level because a microphone produces such a very small voltage it has to be connected to the correct impedance. Occasionally, and particularly with some domestic equipment, other standards of voltage and impedance are found

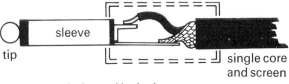

tip

sleeve

single core
and screen

unbalanced jack plug

balanced jack plug

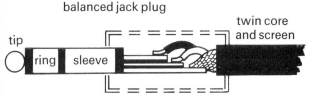

tip

ring sleeve

twin core
and screen

Fig 15 *Wiring of balanced and unbalanced jack plugs*

and equipment using these will not always work satisfactorily with a professional installation. However it may be possible to achieve an acceptable result after some experimentation.

BALANCED OR UNBALANCED

In addition to the voltage and impedance at inputs and outputs of equipment we also need to know whether the connections are 'balanced' or 'unbalanced'. An unbalanced system uses interconnecting cables with one conductor and

Fig 16 *Earth loops causing hum in a balanced system should be broken by disconnecting the screen in one of the plugs. In an unbalanced system all but one of the mains earths* (at the mixer usually) *should be disconnected.* N.B. This should only be done where equipment will not be unplugged from the mixer, thereby breaking the earth connection and making the equipment dangerous.

an overall braided screen (co-axial cable), whereas a balanced system has two conductors plus a screen (twin-screened cable). It follows that plugs and sockets for unbalanced systems need two pins or connections while for a balanced system three are required.

UNBALANCED

Let us look first at the disadvantages of the simpler and cheaper unbalanced system. As stated earlier, the signal voltages used are quite low, just under a volt for line level and about a millivolt for microphone level. All cables will pick up hum and other forms of electrical interference to some extent and there is particular danger at microphone level because the unwanted signal (the interference) may be almost as loud as the wanted signal from the microphone. Even at line level the interfering signals can be much too loud to ignore.

Hum is the most common defect of the unbalanced system and is caused by the electromagnetic radiation or magnetic fields from nearby electrical cables and equipment. Such radiation can have an influence over quite a considerable distance depending upon the type of mains cable, whether it is encased in metal or not, the type of current flowing, etc. The screen of the cable does nothing to eliminate this type of interference — it is there to guard against another kind of interference: electrostatic. The magnetic field induces different voltages in the centre conductor and the surrounding screen and while those induced in the screen have an easy path to earth (ground), those induced in the centre conductor add to the wanted signal.

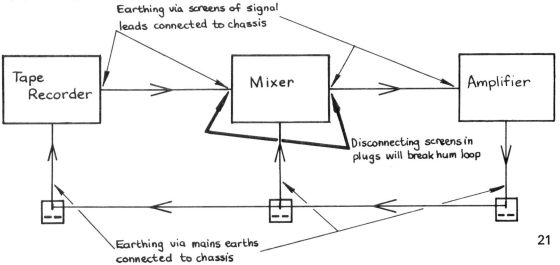

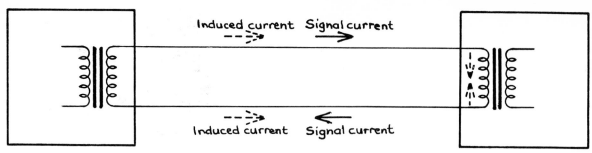

Induced current   Signal current

Induced current   Signal current

Fig 17 *Balancing transformers at either end of an interconnecting cable will make both cores in that cable alike. Similar negative and positive voltages will cancel out induced voltages.*

A further difficulty arises with the interconnection of unbalanced equipment because the screen of the cable which is carrying the signal links the cases of the mixer and amplifier. Both cases should also be connected to earth for safety and there is thus a continuous, circular path from the earth at one mains plug, through the mains cable to the mixer, through the mixer chassis to the screen of the link cable to the amplifier chassis, and thus back to earth via the amplifier mains cable. Although very small, the earth current flowing from the mixer can now divide between its own mains cable route and the route through the screen of the co-axial cable to the earth via the amplifier cable. This earth current combines with the signal in the co-axial cable giving hum in the background of the signal.

We can break the earth loop by disconnecting the earth wire in all but one of the mains plugs. This can be very dangerous but may be justifiable in a fixed installation where the equipment remains *permanently* connected and earthed by the screened cables.

Hum from magnetic fields will not occur because the two conductors are alike (rather than the single conductor and screen forming the circuit in an unbalanced system) and they are also 'balanced'. Balancing is achieved by fitting a transformer at each input and output, as shown in fig. 17, which has the effect of isolating the interconnecting signal wires from the rest of the system. Because the two wires are alike local magnetic fields will induce a similar voltage in each. The wanted signal is flowing round the loop, forwards in one wire and back in the other, but the induced voltage causes currents in the same direction in both wires, say forwards. Thus it adds to one wire and subtracts from the other, giving a net effect of no interference.

So, in order to prevent hum caused by earth loops and magnetic induction a balanced system is preferred, especially for long cable runs. It is sometimes acceptable on the grounds of cost and convenience to use an unbalanced system for linking closely associated pieces of equipment.

BALANCED

With a balanced system this kind of hum loop will not occur because there are two signal wires which are completely independent of the earth (ground) connection. However, a slight hum can still appear via the earth loop formed by the screens of the interconnecting leads and the mains earths. This loop can easily be broken by disconnecting the screen at one end of the cable. Normally this is done at the mixer, which is the central piece of equipment.

RECOMMENDATIONS

Impedances It is now standard practice in broadcasting and other professional organizations for interconnecting circuits to be fed from low impedance outputs to high impedance inputs.

All inputs should be balanced and high impedance, at least 2,000 ohms and preferably 10,000 ohms.

All outputs should be balanced and low impedance, less than 100 ohms.

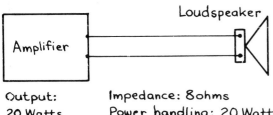

Output:
20 Watts
into 8 ohms

Impedance: 8 ohms
Power handling: 20 Watts

Fig 18 *Correct amplifier loading*

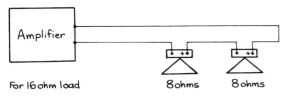

For 16 ohm load   8 ohms   8 ohms

Fig 19 *Loudspeakers wired in series to match amplifier output*

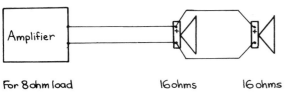

For 8 ohm load   16 ohms   16 ohms

Fig 20 *Loudspeakers wired in parallel to match amplifier output*

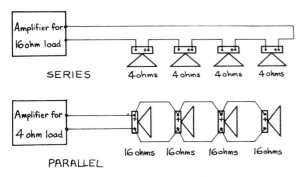

SERIES   4 ohms 4 ohms 4 ohms 4 ohms

PARALLEL   16 ohms 16 ohms 16 ohms 16 ohms

Fig 21 *For N number of loudspeakers of the same impedance Y, in series the combined impedance is N times Y, and in parallel the combined impedance is Y divided by N.*

All inputs and outputs associated with the mixing desk should be at a standard level (zero level) to permit flexibility in their interconnection.

Earthing It is essential that each item of equipment remains earthed either to the mains or via interconnecting screened leads.

LOUDSPEAKER CONNECTION

LOW VOLTAGE SYSTEMS

Loudspeakers have an impedance, which can be somewhere between 2 ohms and 30 ohms, and amplifiers are designed to feed to a specified load, usually of 4, 8 or 16 ohms, so problems may arise in connecting them. Some amplifiers have several outputs to cater for different loads and others have one output with facilities to adjust the correct working load, but usually the manufacturer states, for example, 'Output 20 watts into 8 ohms'. This means that the amplifier will give its optimum performance with a load of 8 ohms, when it will deliver 20 watts.

From an amplifier designed for a loudspeaker of 16 ohms it is possible to run two 8 ohm loudspeakers by wiring them in series to make the total load 16 ohms. Some slight loss of quality will result but for most purposes this is acceptable. Alternatively it is possible to run two 16 ohm loudspeakers from an amplifier designed for a load of 8 ohms by wiring them in parallel. This is a better method of feeding two loudspeakers from one amplifier. The same principles can be applied to a larger number of loudspeakers.

If an amplifier designed for, say, 16 ohms is connected to one of, say, 4 ohms the result will be a louder and perhaps distorted sound, and the amplifier may suffer damage. Conversely, if an amplifier designed for a 4 ohm load is fed to a 16 ohm loudspeaker the result will be a loss of output level.

Although amplifiers can usually accept a load from half to double the one specified, the only sure way of getting reliable results is to follow the manufacturer's instructions. Ideally, where cost is not the determining factor, each loudspeaker should have its own amplifier.

When applied to the requirements of a theatre

installation these restrictions produce three problem areas:

1 Where different combinations of loudspeakers are required to be switched on and off, thereby varying the impedance of the load on the amplifier.

2 Where a large number of loudspeakers are required to operate in a series or series-parallel arrangement, generally producing a high impedance load (for example in a dressing-room paging system).

3 Where long cable runs are required which may result in power being lost in the cable and a worsening of the damping factor (see below).

1 and 2 are usually solved by employing a high voltage system to feed the loudspeakers; the third restriction can also be handled in this way, but the use of cable of sufficient size (i.e. low enough resistance) is usually a satisfactory solution.

DAMPING FACTOR OF LOUDSPEAKER AND AMPLIFIER

Manufacturers of loudspeaker amplifiers usually state a damping factor in addition to the normal load impedance, for example 'Normal load 8 ohms, damping factor 20'. This is a measure of the output impedance of the amplifier itself. Thus,

$$\text{Damping Factor} = \frac{\text{Normal Load Impedance}}{\text{Amplifier Output Impedance}}$$

and in this example

$$20 = \frac{8}{\text{Amplifier Output Impedance}}$$

giving an Output Impedance of 0·4 ohms.

It is important that the impedance 'seen' by the loudspeaker 'looking back' into the amplifier should be as low as possible because the loudspeaker cone is springy in its mounting. If a signal corresponding to a single push of the cone is fed to the amplifier, the cone, of course, moves forward, but when returning to its rest position it can overshoot and oscillate backwards and forwards for a few cycles. This extends the duration of the sound and is a kind of distortion. It must be kept to a minimum by damping the oscillations with as large a damping factor as possible, i.e. as small as possible an impedance seen by the loudspeaker. We saw

above that two 8 ohm loudspeakers could be connected in series and connected to an amplifier designed for 16 ohms. If this amplifier has a damping factor of 20, the amplifier output impedance is $\frac{16}{20}$ or 0·8 ohms. If the diagram is now slightly rearranged (see fig. 22), we find that the impedance seen by the right-hand loudspeaker is now a combination of the amplifier and the left-hand loudspeaker, i.e. 0·8 ohms and 8 ohms. The total impedance seen is 8·8 ohms and the damping factor for the right-hand speaker is $\frac{8}{8·8}$ or 0·9, which degrades the performance rather too much for true high fidelity.

These problems also occur, although to a lesser extent, if the cable used to connect the amplifier to the loudspeaker has too much resistance. In fig. 23 we have a loudspeaker driven over a long run of cable of 1·2 ohm resistance. The loudspeaker now sees a combined impedance of the amplifier output and the cable, i.e. 0·8 + 1·2 or 2 ohms and the damping is reduced from 20 to $\frac{16}{2}$ or 8. Such a reduction would normally be regarded as an acceptable degradation but it is important that the cable is of sufficient size for the intended use.

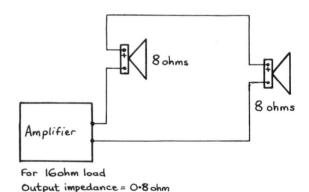

For 16 ohm load
Output impedance = 0·8 ohm

Fig 22 *Loudspeaker damping*

Output impedance = 0·8 ohm   Impedance = 16 ohms

Fig 23 *A cable with too much resistance (i.e. not large enough) can also affect the damping.*

CABLE SIZES IN LOW VOLTAGE SYSTEMS

There is a useful rule of thumb which can be followed to avoid losing too much signal in the cable and making the damping factor too low: this is that the cable resistance should not exceed one tenth of the loudspeaker resistance. If this is kept to the damping factor will not be less than 10 and the signal lost in the cable will not exceed 1 dB.

Thus for an 8 ohm loudspeaker the cable resistance should not exceed 0·8 ohms. On a short run of only a few feet a lightweight cable will be adequate but on longer runs the cable resistance must be considered.

HIGH VOLTAGE SYSTEM

The high voltage system was devised to overcome the many problems which arose with feeding an amplifier directly to several loudspeakers over long cable runs. This method is especially useful in a system utilizing a number of loudspeakers of various types dispersed around a theatre, and when different combinations of loudspeakers are required for each sound effect, etc. The high voltage system is much more flexible, but in a very high quality system the slight limitation of the frequency response at the loudspeakers, caused by the introduction of extra transformers, may not be acceptable. In this case the only solution is to install an amplifier at each loudspeaker and feed at line level to the input of each amplifier. The high voltage system is quite simple and we will first consider feeding from an amplifier to one loudspeaker. Remembering that
watts = volts × amps and volts = amps × ohms, an amplifier designed to feed a 4 ohm loudspeaker with 25 watts is producing 10 volts. As part of the amplifier, a transformer is introduced to step up this voltage to 100 volts, see fig. 24. (In the USA and Canada, also, for safety reasons, in hospitals in the UK, it is more common to use 70 volts.) At the end of the cable run, inside the loudspeaker enclosure, a similar transformer is fitted to step down the 100 volts to 10 volts to feed the loudspeaker itself. The reader may well wonder what has been achieved apart from the purchase of two large and moderately heavy transformers. The advantage is that here we have used a transformer of step-up ratio 10 volts to 100 volts, i.e. 10 times, and a transformer, in stepping up the voltage 10 times, steps up the impedance 100 times, i.e. the square of the voltage ratio. So the output impedance of the amplifier with transformer becomes 100 times greater and the cable resistance is now of much less significance.

Further advantages appear in a system where one amplifier is to feed several loudspeakers, see fig. 25. Here the same amplifier and transformer is used to feed four 6 watt loudspeakers, so that the total load is 24 watts, just inside the capability of the amplifier. The transformers at the loudspeakers are not the same as in the previous example; in this case we have a 6 watt, 4 ohm (say) loudspeaker which requires almost 5 volts to drive it fully and the transformers here have to step down from 100 volts to 5 volts. This is the only way in which four such loudspeakers can be fed from such an amplifier while paying attention to quality, and all the cable can be 'lighting flex' instead of 15 amp cable for a typical length of run in the theatre.

Despite these complications the system is simple to operate. There will be a 100 volt output at the amplifier and there will be a similar input at the loudspeaker. It is usual also to provide at the loudspeaker a means of varying the power taken from the 100 volt line up to the maximum permitted by that particular loudspeaker. Thus a 10 watt-maximum loudspeaker may have settings for 3, 6 and 10 watts. This permits such combinations as shown in fig. 26 which uses six 10 watt units fed from a 40 watt amplifier to cover an auditorium with sound while keeping the source of sound apparently at the front of the hall.

It is important that the amplifier is not overloaded with loudspeakers: a 50 watt amplifier, for example, will not fully drive four loudspeakers set at 25 watts, indeed the amplifier may be damaged by doing so.

This high voltage system has the tremendous advantage of allowing loudspeakers to be switched on and off almost at random without affecting either the amplifier or the remaining loudspeakers. It also permits the development of systems in which several amplifiers can be fed to any of a number of loudspeakers. It is, of course, essential that the switching does not allow the outputs of two amplifiers to be connected together.

Fig 24 *Feeding a loudspeaker at a high voltage to ensure that there is no loss of impedance on a long cable run.*

25 Watt Loudspeaker

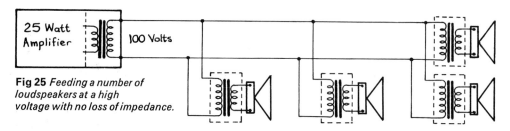

Fig 25 *Feeding a number of loudspeakers at a high voltage with no loss of impedance.*

4 Loudspeakers ; each 6 Watts power handling

Transformers set at 10 Watts

Fig 26 *One 40 watt amplifier feeding two 10 watt capacity loudspeakers at 10 watts each for maximum efficiency, and four 10 watt capacity loudspeakers at 5 watts each to obtain less output.*

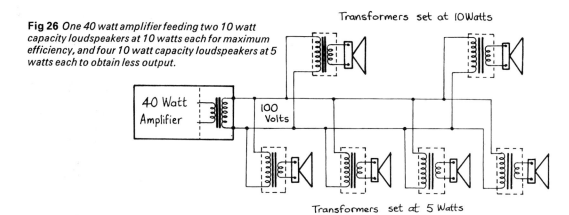

Transformers set at 5 Watts

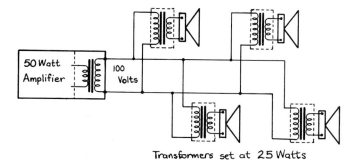

Transformers set at 25 Watts

Fig 27 *Overloading of amplifier output (example A)*

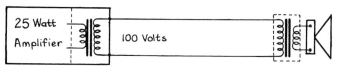

Transformer set at 50 Watts

Fig 28 *Overloading of amplifier output (example B)*

3 Loudspeakers

A loudspeaker is in many ways the reverse of a microphone. Its purpose is to create movements of air by the controlled oscillation of a cone or diaphragm, thereby manufacturing sound pressure waves.

The size of the loudspeaker is a determining factor in the frequency range it will reproduce. A deep bass sound requires a large area of air moving slowly, while a high frequency sound is produced by a smaller area of air moving rapidly. Hence the need for large cone loudspeakers ('woofers') of up to 15 in. or 18 in. (380 or 457 mm) in diameter and small 'tweeters' down to $1\frac{1}{2}$ in. or 2 in. (37 or 50 mm). Sometimes a loudspeaker cabinet contains an intermediate size of loudspeaker suited to handling the mid-frequency range.

A cross-over (or dividing) network is necessary to segregate the range of frequencies and to allow the most efficient operation of the loudspeakers. This network also protects the units, as a tweeter could be damaged when trying to cope with powerful bass sounds. A complete loudspeaker system operates rather like a choir where the soprano never gets the bass or baritone parts and vice versa but she will overlap slightly with the contralto who will overlap slightly with the tenor, and so on (see photograph 3).

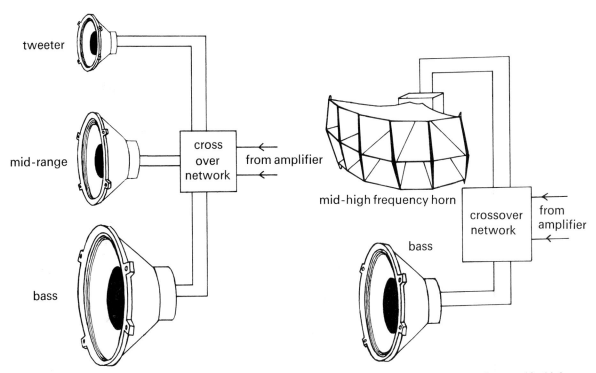

Fig 29 *Loudspeaker arrangement commonly used for high fidelity systems.*

Fig 30 *Loudspeaker arrangement often used for high intensity sound.*

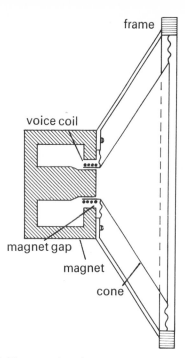

frame

voice coil

magnet gap

magnet

cone

Fig 31 *The operation of a cone loudspeaker*

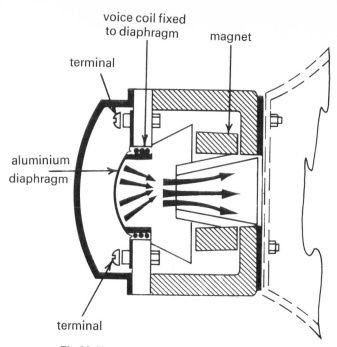

voice coil fixed
to diaphragm

magnet

terminal

aluminium
diaphragm

terminal

Fig 32 *Horn pressure unit. The aluminium diaphragm is capable of a much greater intensity of mid/high frequencies than a paper cone. A horn is fixed on the front to direct the sound.*

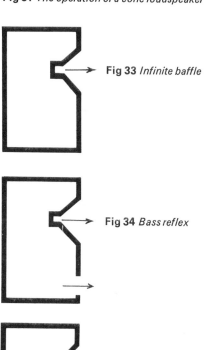

Fig 33 *Infinite baffle*

Fig 34 *Bass reflex*

Fig 35 *Back loaded horn or folded horn*

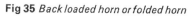

Back loaded
or Folded horn

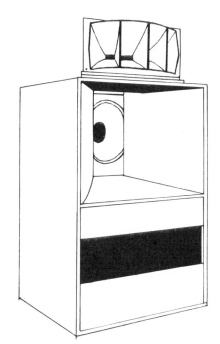

Fig 36 *Combination of bass reflex and front loaded horn cabinet together with a mid/high frequency horn unit as seen in the famous Altec 'Voice of the Theatre' loudspeaker.*

HOW IT WORKS

A loudspeaker is very similar in operation and construction to a moving-coil microphone. A metal voice coil is fixed rigidly to the diaphragm. The ends of this coil are connected to an amplifier from which they receive alternating voltages. These cause the voice coil to move within the surrounding magnet. The oscillation of the voice coil causes the movement of the diaphragm which produces sound waves in the air.

With a cone loudspeaker, the cone which is attached to the coil is usually made of a paper composition and is therefore very delicate. The outer rim of the cone is attached to the loudspeaker frame with a flexible material which allows the necessary play.

With a horn loudspeaker, which provides a much greater intensity of mid and high frequency sound, something more robust than a paper cone is necessary. In this case the voice coil is attached to an aluminium disc or diaphragm. This is called a pressure unit and is built into a casing with the magnet.

CABINETS OR 'ENCLOSURES'

Every cone loudspeaker has to be mounted somehow and the enclosure is as important a part of the system as the loudspeaker itself. A properly designed cabinet cannot make a poorly designed speaker operate satisfactorily, nor can a well designed speaker perform efficiently when housed in an inferior enclosure. The speaker and the enclosure must be of good design and work together as a unit. The prime reason for an enclosure or baffle is to separate the sound radiated from the rear of a speaker diaphragm or cone so that it does not cancel the radiation generated by the front of the cone.

Broadly speaking a large loudspeaker unit of excellent quality is better than a small one. Similarly, a large enclosure of good design is better than a small one. Before discussing enclosures, however, one must understand the basic differences between the four major categories, which are as follows:

1 *Infinite baffles* A true example of an infinite baffle is where a speaker is mounted through a wall with the front of the diaphragm radiating into the listening room and the rear of the diaphragm radiating into the room on the other side of the wall.

This type of enclosure is generally not feasible so we compromise by completely enclosing the speaker in a box and calling that an infinite baffle. However, the volume of air that is trapped in such a box constitutes an added 'stiffness' to the physical operation of the loudspeaker and this has the effect of restricting the bass response. A properly designed infinite baffle, taking this into account, is necessarily a large enclosure.

2 *Bass reflex enclosures* These consist of an enclosed volume with a port opening.

We originally enclosed the speaker to stop the low frequency sound radiating from the rear of the cone 'flowing' round and cancelling out the front radiations. A bass reflex enclosure will make use of these low frequency radiations which would otherwise be absorbed in the box.

In order to do this the distance of the port from the cone is calculated so that the sound arrives broadly out of phase with the rear of the cone. It is thus in phase with the sound from the front of the cone and will add to it. In this way the bass response, which was restricted in the infinite baffle, is now enhanced.

3 *Low frequency horns* This type of enclosure serves two purposes. It permits the cone to radiate normally at all frequencies as it does in an infinite baffle. It also reinforces the bass by utilizing the back radiation from the cone as described in the bass reflex cabinet, only this time the bass is projected by means of a horn.

Because bass frequencies have long wavelengths (6 feet (2 m) and more) the horn must have a comparable dimension, and to conserve space it is usually folded within the cabinet. However, with a low frequency horn enclosure it is difficult to avoid phase differences between the high and low frequencies which could be undesirable.

4 *Combination enclosures* Combinations of the bass reflex and horn enclosures can be very effective. The advantages of the extended bass response of the bass reflex enclosure, coupled to a short front loaded horn without folds, gives extended bass response without phase errors.

Cost and size In the theatre we are usually concerned with maximum sound pressure levels (loudness) coupled with a broad and uniform frequency response (quality). Unfortunately, this means large cost and sizeable units.

A fair comparison would be to take the hi-fi loudspeakers you have at home; try dividing the volume of the theatre by the volume of your room, then multiplying the size of your loudspeakers by the result. Use the same factor to multiply the cost and you will get a fair idea of what should be spent on theatre loudspeakers.

Power handling capacity The power handling capacity of a loudspeaker, that is, how many watts received from the amplifier it will cope with successfully, is a guide to the achievable 'loudness' of the unit. However, some loudspeakers are so designed that they are not very efficient. Therefore it is important to investigate for comparison with other units the published figures given for sound pressure levels.

It is generally advisable to allow for a larger power in the loudspeaker than that normally supplied by the power amplifier. The reason for this is that while overload of the amplifier results in distortion, overload of the loudspeaker may result in burnout or other physical damage. It is wise therefore to match a 35 watt amplifier with a loudspeaker capable of withstanding a constant electrical power of 35 watts and intermittent peaks of 50 watts. This would

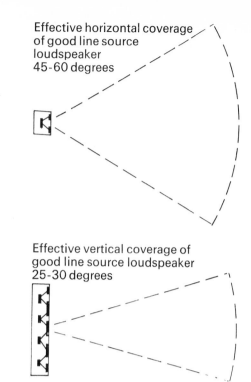

Fig 38 *Coverage of columnar loudspeaker*

be stated as 35 watts RMS (Root Mean Square, a standard means of measuring the *effective* current) and 50 watts peak.

Remember that in 100 volt (or 70 volt) systems a stepdown transformer will be required with the loudspeaker. And this must be of the correct rating. (See Chapter 2.)

Conformity All enclosures have their own particular characteristics so it is desirable that, as far as possible, one type of loudspeaker and enclosure is used throughout the entire sound system. In this way the 'voice' of the sound will not undergo distracting changes when moved from one loudspeaker to another.

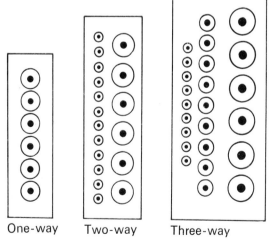

One-way Two-way Three-way

Fig 37 *The Bozak range of columnar loudspeakers provide a wide horizontal and narrow vertical coverage by virtue of the number of cone units in each column. The two-way column incorporates separate low and high frequency units for increased frequency response.*

PHASING

When connecting up loudspeakers it is of prime importance to observe the correct phasing. In simple terms, all the 'positive' connections on the amplifier and loudspeakers should be wired to, say, the red wire and all the 'negative' connections wired to the black one.

If this is not scrupulously checked loudspeakers may be working out of phase, i.e. when one cone is moving forwards in its oscillating cycle the other is moving backwards. The result is a cancelling effect which reduces the bass response and also the apparent level when the listener is standing between the two loudspeakers.

DIRECTIVITY

When dealing with speech reinforcement and public address systems directivity becomes a key factor. To achieve a uniform coverage of an auditorium with maximum potential gain before feedback or howl round from the microphones, directional microphones are used to point at the stage and directional loudspeakers are used to point at the audience.

The first rule to remember is that only high frequencies are directional. The bass tends to spread around in an uncontrollable fashion. Fortunately the 'speech intelligibility' frequencies or the 'presence' frequencies are in the higher range, and this factor can be used to advantage.

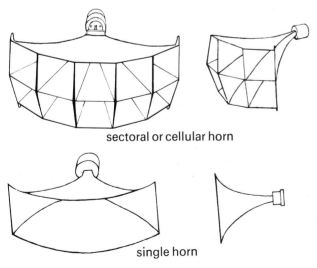

sectoral or cellular horn

single horn

Fig 39 *Horn loudspeakers*

There are two methods of obtaining directivity in a loudspeaker. The first is by using a high frequency pressure unit driving into a horn, the size and shape of the horn determining the distribution pattern. The second is by placing loudspeakers, one above the other, in a column or line.

Line source loudspeakers It is a physical fact that each time you place a like loudspeaker on top of another you decrease the vertical distribution, concentrating more power in the horizontal plane.

A line source loudspeaker is a column of cone units (usually) mounted in an infinite baffle enclosure. The resulting HF distribution pattern is fan-shaped in the horizontal plane with striking and definite perimeters. With some hiss through the system you can test this for yourself by finding where the sound sharply drops away. With a good line source unit it will be noticeable within a matter of inches.

The other great advantage of this type of loudspeaker is that, when correctly positioned, the maximum power output can be directed at the rear of an auditorium while the front rows are only receiving the benefit of the lower one or two cone units in the cabinet. The farther back you go the more benefit you receive from the loudspeaker.

High frequency dispersal horns The main advantages of using combinations of directional horn loudspeakers in conjunction with separate bass units are frequency response and power. There is no substitute for a properly designed bass enclosure for power and performance, and a pressure unit is capable of handling more HF signal than an ordinary cone.

The disadvantages of this arrangement are size and quality. It is not always physically possible to mount large bass enclosures in an auditorium, and even if it is possible it is aesthetically not as pleasing as slim column loudspeakers.

As far as quality goes, it is possible to use the very best cone units in a column (although many manufacturers do not do so in the interests of economy), whereas it is difficult to produce a 'sweet' sounding HF horn. The nature of the beast is to be on the hard side, and where power and definition are required this is a distinct advantage. For normal use, tone controls will help produce a more pleasant sound.

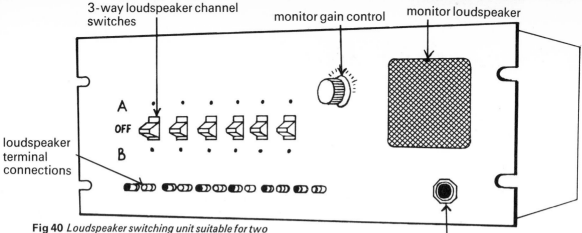

3-way loudspeaker channel switches

monitor gain control

monitor loudspeaker

loudspeaker terminal connections

Fig 40 *Loudspeaker switching unit suitable for two amplifiers feeding any combination of up to six loudspeakers via 100 volts line.*

alternative headset socket

There are various types of horn loudspeaker. The sectoral or cellular horn is useful because the distribution pattern remains constant over a wide frequency range, and there is good scope for conveniently increasing the coverage to a known degree by adding to the number of cells.

USES

It is difficult to be specific but in general I would choose loudspeaker systems as follows:

Line source
Subtle speech reinforcement in an auditorium. Low to medium intensity music and sound effects.
Very reverberant conditions where directivity is critical to minimize the proliferation of sound paths which would cause more echoes.

Bass units and HF horns
Speech reinforcement in large auditoria.
Playback of loud music and effects in any situation.
Playback of effects from back stage where additional HF will be required because the speakers are masked by scenery.
High intensity microphone work, e.g. pop concerts.

LOUDSPEAKER SWITCHING

Each loudspeaker or group of loudspeakers is associated to a power amplifier. If that power amplifier fails it is an advantage to be able to switch immediately to a standby. To do this a suitable number of routing push buttons or rotary selector switches must be incorporated. The switching system must be designed within the following guide lines:

1 The amplifier must not be overloaded beyond its wattage capability by haphazard loudspeaker routing.

2 The amplifier must not be presented with incorrect impedances.

3 It must be impossible to connect more than one amplifier to any speaker or group of speakers.

4 It must be impossible for any amplifier to be left without some form of load on the output. This need not necessarily be a loudspeaker, it can be what is known as a 'dummy load' in the form of correct value resistors. Hence, when a loudspeaker is rerouted the switching arrangement should cater for a dummy load to take its place.

SWITCHING AT LINE LEVEL

Switching to change location in a sound effects system is technically best handled when there is an amplifier for every loudspeaker. In this case the switching can be done between the mixer and the amplifier at line level. As much routing as possible should be done at low level where it is easy to avoid impedance mismatching and electrical 'splats' which often occur at loudspeaker levels.

4 Power amplifiers

A power amplifier takes a line level signal and amplifies it to a degree where it is powerful enough to make a loudspeaker respond. Without going into technicalities there is not a great deal one can add to what has been said in previous chapters about amplifiers. They come in many shapes and sizes with varying inputs and power ratings. Each year smaller and more powerful amplifiers come on to the market with the advances in circuitry and transistor design (photograph 5).

INPUT

Straight amplifiers will have a line level input which in most cases will be unbalanced as they are usually closely associated to the mixer and long leads are not necessary.

OUTPUTS

The output impedance will be stated and/or there may be a 100 volt output. In some cases there will be a choice of impedances, for example, 4, 8 and 16 ohms (photograph 6).

POWER RATING

The unit will have a power rating which is stated in two ways: the continuous maximum power it will happily generate over a reasonable frequency range given an unvarying 0 dB signal (RMS), and the maximum burst of power it will handle above that figure when fed with a normal varying programme (this is known as a music or peak figure). The RMS figure is the more important one.

MIXER/AMPLIFIERS

Some amplifiers have inputs with gain and tone controls for microphones or other equipment. In other words, there is a mixer incorporated. These mixer/amplifiers are mainly used for small permanent or portable P.A. systems and can be very useful for rehearsal purposes (photograph 7).

5 Mixers

A mixer accepts a number of signals from varying sources, provides each with a volume control for 'balancing' purposes and sends out the blended result as one line level signal. In addition, tone controls may be added either to each individual input channel or, more simply, to the overall blended signal.

A stereo mixer has two separate outputs. Associated with each input channel is a two-way fader called a 'pan' control which can be adjusted to send the signal to the left output, the right output or anywhere in between. Less sophisticated systems use a three-way switch giving left, right or both outputs (photographs 8 and 9).

ESSENTIALS

The mixer is the heart of any sound system and should therefore:

1 be to the highest technical standard of performance,

2 be as flexible as possible (i.e. interchangeability of types of input via plugging, switching, exchange of modules, etc.),

3 be straightforward to operate and positioned correctly,

4 incorporate as many 'extras' as the budget will allow.

EXTRAS

The 'extras' (although some might be thought essential) could be listed in approximate order of importance as follows:

1 Linear instead of rotary faders (for more precise operation).

2 VU meters (for visual check on overdriving the system: also for recording purposes).

3 Individual bass, mid and treble controls for each channel. (A mid frequency boost particularly accentuates the voice frequencies, making them appear to 'stand out'. Hence, this function is sometimes called presence. A sophisticated mixer will have presence in different bands to cater for a range of voices and instruments) (photograph 11).

4 Microphone/line inputs on each channel (switchable or pluggable).

5 Microphone input sensitivity control (to allow for high or low gain from the microphones) (photograph 10).

6 Echo or reverberation controls (the reverberation unit is an external addition).

7 Pre-fade listen (PFL). This is a key on each channel which allows you to listen to that channel via a monitor headset or loudspeaker when the fader is down or in the off position. It is especially useful for cueing up or checking tapes, and for checking that microphones are properly connected and operating.

8 Foldback. This is a facility with separate gain controls on each channel which allow a blend of chosen signals arriving into the desk to be fed back (or folded back) to the stage area. Foldback is received either on headsets or on loudspeakers via an amplifier. In the latter case feedback is an obvious hazard. Foldback is used a great deal in recording studios where, for instance, a drummer surrounded by acoustic screens is unable to hear the other instruments clearly. In this case one might feed into his headsets the piano and lead guitar who are playing the melody line, plus the vocalist. Then, as he is wearing cans, he might ask for the addition of his own microphones so that he can hear what he is doing.

In a theatre situation it usually means that the voices on stage are folded back to the musicians and the musicians in the pit are folded back to the stage. Often a singer on stage using a microphone will say that he cannot hear himself. This is because all the loudspeakers are directed away from him. A little judicious foldback will make him feel more secure.

There is a growing tendency in big musicals and revues to use a combination of live sound and microphones, with tape recordings to which the artistes mime. This not only provides a more pleasing sound but allows the people on stage more freedom of movement. Tape foldback is an essential part of this operation.

MIXING CONSOLES

Large permanent installations often have the mixer built into a console which includes all the ancillary facilities like loudspeaker switching, microphone and loudspeaker plug patch panels, tape remote controls, cuelights and intercommunication.

Photograph 13 shows an example of such a console. The mixer in this instance does not have 'panning' to two stereo outputs (or groups, so called because they become groups of input channels), but has push-button selection to six output groups. Each output, via its own fader, feeds into a 100 watt amplifier. The first two drive the two sets of proscenium loudspeakers and are thus correctly matched for power and impedance. The second two drive a limited number of 'selectable' loudspeakers in the auditorium and the last pair drive selectable loudspeakers on stage. Splitting up the groups in this fashion provides a greater flexibility of operation with less chance of loading any amplifier with too many loudspeakers. The plug patch panel caters for 'overplugging' should any group need to be used for other purposes; for example, two extra loudspeakers on stage replacing those on the proscenium. This would provide four individual sound locations in the stage area, each with a gain control and each capable of receiving any one or any combination of sound sources fed into the mixing desk. Thus a single taped effect of, say, a motor cycle can be 'moved' around the stage.

6 Echo and reverberation

Echo can be obtained by means of the record and playback heads on a tape machine. Take a straight signal, feed it also to a tape machine which is recording, take the signal from the playback head and mix it with the original and the result is tape delay echo.

Especially made tape delay machines have a number of replay heads which provide a series of echoes. These devices often use an endless loop of tape rather than reel to reel (photograph 14).

For reverberation a different system is employed. A portion of the straight signal is sent to what is virtually the driving mechanism of a loudspeaker. This is attached to either one end of a long coiled spring (photograph 15) or, more expensively, to a large sheet of thin steel called a plate (photograph 16). The coil or plate is caused to vibrate and each vibration takes a certain amount of time to ripple along the length. At the other end a magnetic pick-up (as used in a gramophone pick-up) reacts to these delayed vibrations and sends them back to be mixed in with the original signal. Some degree of equalization (tone correction) is usually incorporated to obtain optimum quality from what is basically a crude device.

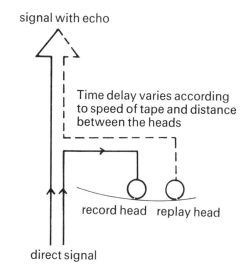

Fig 41 *Tape delay echo*

Fig 42 *A portion of the signal at any input channel is sent to the echo unit and returns to be mixed back into the final output.*

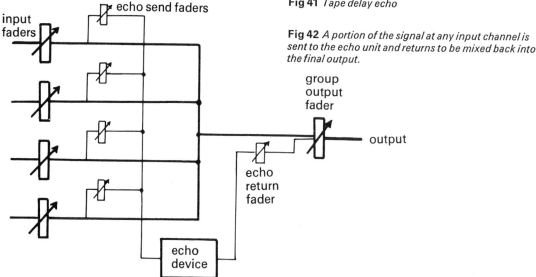

7 Disc replay

A disc replay (or playback) unit operates on the (by now familiar) principle of vibrations being turned into electrical impulses. The stylus sits in the groove of a revolving disc. The groove has a varying lateral pattern which the stylus is forced to follow and which causes it to vibrate; these vibrations are turned into tiny electrical currents by one of several methods depending upon the type of pick-up.

I shall not go very deeply into the technicalities of disc reproduction here. Suffice it to say that a gramophone pick-up is very similar in operation to a microphone, which is discussed in the next chapter.

THE TURNTABLE

The essence of a good turntable is that it should run accurately at the set speed with no fluctuations and that the motor should not cause vibrations which can affect the pick-up, thereby causing an unacceptable low frequency rumble (photograph 17).

The unit should also be mounted so that any vibrations in the room such as footsteps, doors shutting, etc., will not be transmitted to the pick-up. Even a heavy tread on a wooden floor can make a modern lightweight pick-up arm jump a groove. The remedy is either very solid mounting or, at the other extreme, a sprung mounting, in which the springs upon which the unit sits will absorb any shocks.

Speeds of $33\frac{1}{2}$ and 45 r.p.m. are essential and 78 r.p.m. is useful for old recordings. A constantly variable speed facility is invaluable, especially for making up sound effects; a bell can be slowed down to lower the pitch, a wind effect can be speeded up to make it sound stronger, etc.

The pick-up arm Some turntables come with their own arms and also incorporate a lowering device, a sensible addition which saves many a cracked groove (photograph 18).

If a separate arm is required choose one that is reasonably robust and has a counterweighted balance which can be adjusted to the correct weight for the cartridge. With old 78s (which require a different cartridge) or worn discs the reproduction is sometimes improved by slightly increasing the weight.

Pick-ups Crystal, ceramic, moving coil and semi-conductor pick-ups are all devices for turning vibrations into voltages. It is generally accepted that a crystal pick-up while being both cheap and robust does not provide the frequency range desirable in a first-class system. I would tend to go for a high quality moving coil with a diamond stylus – as this will last longer and be less damaging than a sapphire.

PREAMPLIFIER

It is good practice to incorporate a preamplifier into the disc unit, bringing the output of the pick-up head up to line level (photograph 18). It then becomes another standard item which can be used anywhere in the system.

Certain tone controls are particularly relevant to discs so it is convenient both operationally and electronically to incorporate them here. The basics are a 'scratch' filter (which just removes the higher frequencies) and boost and cut of bass and treble. A more sophisticated unit would include:

1 Rumble filter. A switch which rolls away the bass below a certain frequency (usually about 60 Hz).
2 High frequency filters. Normally a choice of three frequencies (e.g. 5 KHz, 7 KHz, 10 KHz).
3 Slope control. This determines how sharply the HF rolls away at the selected frequency.
4 Treble boost and cut.
5 Bass boost and cut.

It is also useful to have a Master Gain control, a headset socket which remains unaffected by the Master Gain (for cueing up discs), and a Mono/Stereo selector switch.

8 Microphones

A microphone is a device for converting acoustic power (sound pressure waves) into electrical power which has essentially similar wave characteristics. It is very similar to the human ear in many ways, the 'diaphragm' performing the same function as the ear drum (photograph 20).

There are five kinds of microphone:

1 *Carbon microphone* The sound pressure waves acting upon the diaphragm compress the carbon granules, thereby producing an alternating electric resistance which modulates the current supplied by the battery (or by a low voltage mains supply). This system is still used today in the microphone part of a telephone. Carbon microphones are very robust but do not have directional properties and the frequency range is very limited. They are certainly not suitable for any form of 'quality' transmission.

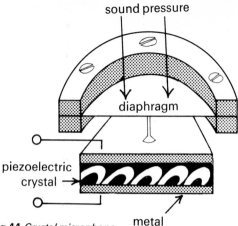

Fig 44 *Crystal microphone*

2 *Crystal microphone* The diaphragm presses against 'piezoelectric' crystals, deforming them so that they generate an alternating voltage. This is again a non-directional limited frequency range device. Since crystal microphones are robust, a convenient size and cheap to produce they are sold a great deal with the smaller domestic tape recorders.

3 *Ribbon microphone* A 'ribbon' made of a corrugated strip of metal foil is fixed at each end to be between the poles of a magnet. The sound pressure waves move the ribbon in the magnetic field between the poles of the magnet, generating a small alternating voltage between the ends of the ribbon. Ribbon microphones are usually sensitive front and back and relatively 'dead' on the sides. Good ribbon microphones

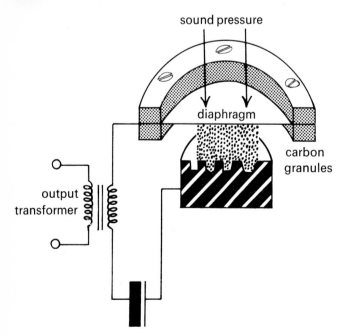

Fig 43 *Carbon microphone*

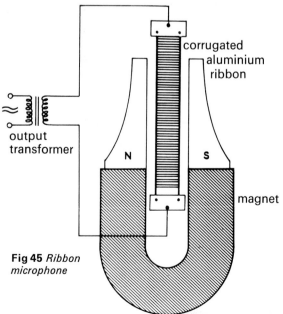

Fig 45 *Ribbon microphone*

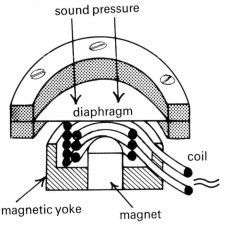

Fig 46 *Dynamic moving coil microphone*

are used in broadcasting and recording studios. The nature of their construction makes them fairly delicate and simply blowing on one can, and probably will, cause damage. They are medium priced.

4 *Dynamic moving coil microphone* A metal coil rigidly fixed to the diaphragm moves in a magnetic field inducing a small current in the coil. Dynamic microphones, depending upon their design, can have any form of directivity of pick-up although they are most commonly found either with an all round pick-up (omni-directional) or with one very definite live side (directional). The quality of the best of these microphones is excellent and they are reasonably robust.

5 *Condenser microphone* A thin diaphragm which forms one electrode of a condenser vibrates close to a fixed counter-electrode, thus producing variations in the capacitance (or impedance) of the condenser. The condenser is given a constant charge via a very high resistance and this produces a voltage between the

Fig 47 *Condenser microphone*

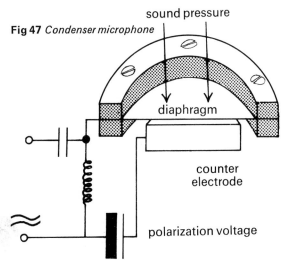

plates of the condenser. This voltage varies with the changes in capacitance caused by the sound waves. It follows that a condenser micro-phone requires a power source to make it oper-ate. A good condenser microphone is of the highest quality attainable. They are more expen-sive than most other microphones and require gentle handling.

DIRECTIVITY

One of the big drawbacks of a microphone is that it 'hears' everything (within the boundaries of its design and construction). That is why so

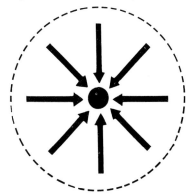

Fig 48 *Omnidirectional pattern*

much care is taken to ensure that recording studios are absolutely silent and sound-proof against outside noise, and that the acoustics are favourable to recording techniques. Largely because of this lack of discrimination, micro-phones have been developed with differing directional characteristics to compensate for various conditions. They may be categorized as follows:

1 *Omnidirectional* Also known as nondirec-tional. The microphone is equally sensitive in all directions. This is useful for, say, picking up a group of voices. Omnidirectional microphones are also used as 'chest' or 'lavalier' microphones attached to a halter hung round the neck of the speaker. Often to obviate the need for a trailing lead they are fed into miniature portable radio transmitters concealed on the person. An 'Omni' is preferred in this instance because of the proximity to, and the constant movement of the head. An omnidirectional microphone is not to be recommended for use in close proximity to loudspeakers where feedback is a problem;

Fig 49 *Bidirectional pattern*

neither should it be used in reverberant conditions as it will pick up all the unwanted sounds.
2 *Bidirectional* Also known as 'figure of eight', for obvious reasons. The pick-up pattern takes the form of a 'live ball' at the front and rear of the microphone with relative deadness at the sides, top and bottom. The pattern can vary with different makes of microphone; some are more sensitive at the front than the rear and most are remarkably dead at the sides.

Bidirectional microphones are useful for picking up speakers each side of the microphone or for recording instruments, e.g. strings, where you require the direct sound from the instrument plus some room acoustic to liven it up a little.

They are also extremely effective for broadcast drama work where an actor can seem to be walking into the distance merely by moving a few inches on to the dead side of the microphone.

front compared to the rear. One of the variations is the hypercardioid or the supercardioid which has a narrower front lobe with a slight rear pick-up but it is extremely dead to sound from lateral sources.

This type of microphone is, perhaps, the most useful in a live performance situation because of its exclusion of unwanted sounds and the possibility of keeping the dead side to the loud-speakers to minimize feedback. Directional microphones are also used extensively in recording studios to obtain maximum 'separation' between instruments.

A word about rifle or gun microphones: I would like to explode the myth that it is possible for a spy to set up an ultra-sensitive rifle microphone outside a window half a mile away and pick up a conversation inside the building. Theatre directors are constantly asking me to obtain one of these devices in order to amplify a singer thirty foot up stage on a twelve foot high rostrum – the sad truth is that this is still pure science fiction. However, gun microphones do exist. They are basically good directional microphones with perforated extension tubes on the front which are so designed that the higher frequencies are rejected from the sides, giving the effect of more directivity.

The unit can only be effectively used about three times farther away from the sound source than an ordinary cardioid microphone.

Fig 50 *Cardioid pattern (directional)*

3 *Directional* Also known as unidirectional or cardioid. The word 'cardioid' derives from the heart-shaped pick-up pattern. The shape of the pattern varies with the make of microphone but a good cardioid is extremely sensitive at the

Fig 51 *Hypercardioid pattern (very directional but with increased sensitivity at rear)*

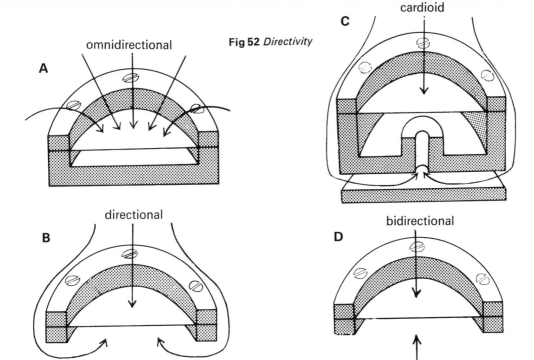

omnidirectional

A

directional

B

cardioid

C

bidirectional

D

Fig 52 *Directivity*

HOW DIRECTIVITY IS ACCOMPLISHED

A If only one side of a diaphragm is exposed to the sound source while the other side is sealed against the environment, sound pressure waves from all directions will move the diaphragm with equal intensity making it an omnidirectional microphone.

B If both the front and rear of the diaphragm are exposed to the sound field, the force moving the diaphragm is due to the difference in the sound pressures in front and behind the diaphragm. This difference produces a directional effect.

C If both the front and rear are exposed to the sound field but the construction of the microphone is such that the pressure waves reaching the rear are delayed by a scientifically calculated amount of time (i.e. inverting the phase) then the result is a cardioid response.

D If both sides of the diaphragm are equally exposed to the sound field the result will be a figure-of-eight pattern (bidirectional effect).

CABLES AND CONNECTORS

Microphone cables must be twin core for the go and return and they must have lap-wound or braided screening with an overall PVC insulat-

ing sheath. Twin 14/0·0076 (metric equivalent: 13/0·2) colour coded and screened PVC (or rubber) covered cable is recommended for most applications.

Since microphone cables are particularly susceptible to all forms of electrical interference, great care must be taken to keep them well clear of all mains cables and control gear and even from other audio wiring, especially high voltage speaker cables.

Connectors should be very robust, incorporating a 'solid' connection. Flimsy contacts can cause problems.

Tip, ring and sleeve (3 pole) jack plugs are often used as they are conveniently sized and priced. However, dirt can be a hazard with this form of connector; a small spot of grease or a little dust can produce a faulty connection.

Cannon XLR 3-pin plugs and sockets are recommended where possible.

IMPEDANCE

High impedance microphones should not be used in a properly engineered system. Apart from their greater susceptibility to interference, the capacitance in a long cable run at high impedance seriously reduces the microphone's high frequency response.

9 The tape recorder

THE MACHINE

A tape recorder is a device for recording, storing and subsequently reproducing sound. The storage medium is a continuous strip of material capable of being magnetized (tape) which is drawn at a constant speed across a recording head. Also known as a magnetic head, this is an electro-magnet consisting of a coil of wire on an iron core with an extremely narrow gap. Sound waves translated into electrical impulses or voltages via a microphone are first amplified by the record amplifier and then fed to the recording head. A magnetic field, the intensity of which varies synchronously with the original sound waves, develops across the gap in the head. The tape travelling past the head becomes magnetized to a greater or lesser extent dependent upon the variation in this intensity. Therefore the intensity variation of the magnetization on the tape becomes a representation of the original sound waves.

Fig 54 *Record head*

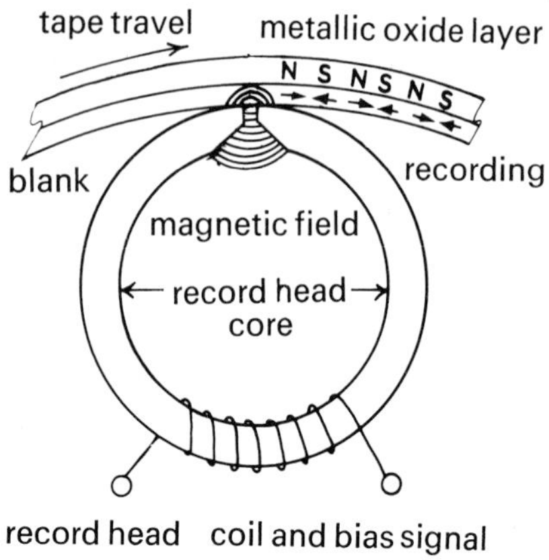

tape travel

metallic oxide layer

N S N S N S

blank

recording

magnetic field

record head core

record head coil and bias signal

Fig 55 *Erase head*

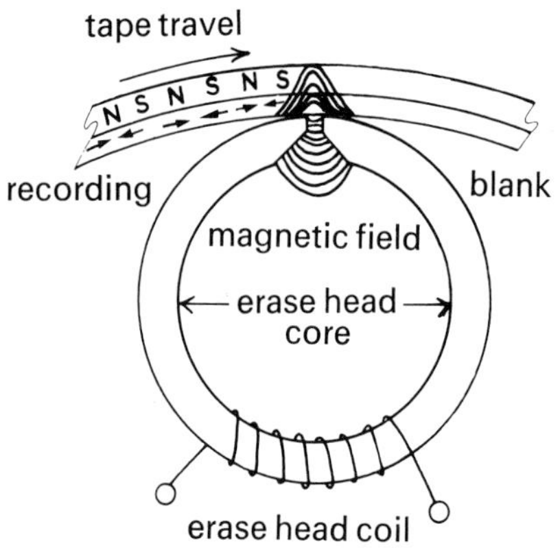

tape travel

N S N S N S

recording

blank

magnetic field

erase head core

erase head coil

Fig 53 *Layout of heads on a normal three head recorder*

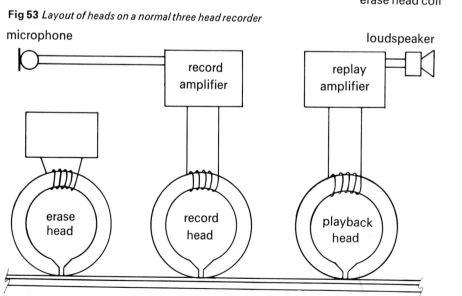

microphone

record amplifier

loudspeaker

replay amplifier

erase head

record head

playback head

tape travel

BIAS

In order to obtain a recording that is distortion-free, the tape must also be magnetized by a high frequency bias signal. Magnetic tape does not respond in an even and predictable way unless there is a certain minimum magnetic force from the recording head. The bias signal provides this minimum force at an ultrasonic frequency of between 40,000 Hz and 80,000 Hz. It only becomes audible if the tape recorder is faulty and in need of adjustment.

PLAYBACK

The playback process is pretty well the reverse of the recording process. The tape is drawn past the playback head at exactly the same speed as when it was recorded and the varying intensities of magnetism on the tape induce corresponding voltages in the coil via the magnetic flux in the head. This pattern of voltages is then amplified by the playback amplifier and fed to a loudspeaker. The loudspeaker converts the electrical impulses into sound waves and the cycle is complete. On the cheaper domestic machines the same head and amplifier double for both the record and replay processes. In this case a suitable switching system is incorporated.

ERASE

Once recorded a tape can be used many times with no significant deterioration provided it is stored in a reasonable temperature and not exposed to other magnetic fields.

But one of the attractions of tape is that it is simple to remove the original information and replace it with a new recording. For this purpose an erase head is incorporated into the system to clear the tape of any programme material before it reaches the recording head. The erase head produces a magnetic field induced by an ultrasonic alternating current that flows through the windings of the coil. This action demagnetizes the tape and the original recording disappears. Naturally, the erase head only comes into operation when one is recording. On playback the erase head is automatically switched off.

THE BASIC SYSTEM

The basic system consists of two main sections – one mechanical and one electronic.

The mechanical section, or tape-drive mechanism transports the tape past the magnetic heads at a precisely controlled speed. The minutest variation of speed is noticeable in the form of an irregularity in the sound, often called 'wow' or 'flutter'. This same mechanism also accomplishes the high-speed rewinding of the tape. The capstan maintains a constant tape speed. The tape is kept in pressure contact with the capstan, which is a revolving shaft, by means of a pinch wheel. The diameter and the number of revolutions per minute of the capstan control the tape speed. The tape is drawn from the left-hand spool across the heads by the capstan and pinch wheel roller. The right-hand spool then takes up the slack tape as it leaves the capstan. This spool is driven either by a separate motor or by a belt drive from the capstan motor. For rewind purposes the supply spool is either driven by a third motor or again belt driven from the capstan. A three-motor transport is a better system. A set of tape guides is usually placed on either side of the head so that the height of the tape is kept at the same level to ensure the correct positioning of the tracks during recording and playback. Close contact between the tape and the magnetic head is achieved either by the tape tension alone or by a system of pressure pads. Most recorders are equipped with tape indicators or tape counters with which particular points in a recording may be located. These counters are coupled to the shaft of one of the reels and therefore do not indicate the footage of the tape itself or the playing time. However, they are accurate enough to find any desired spot on the tape, provided that the same type and thickness of tape with the same inside diameter of reel are employed both in recording and playback. Professional machines are often provided with fairly accurate counters which clock up the minutes and seconds.

The electronic section consists of an amplifier for the recording and reproducing process, recording level controls and an oscillator circuit which produces the high frequency current for the ultrasonic bias and the erasure.

Because of physical factors involved in the magnetic recording process, the low and high

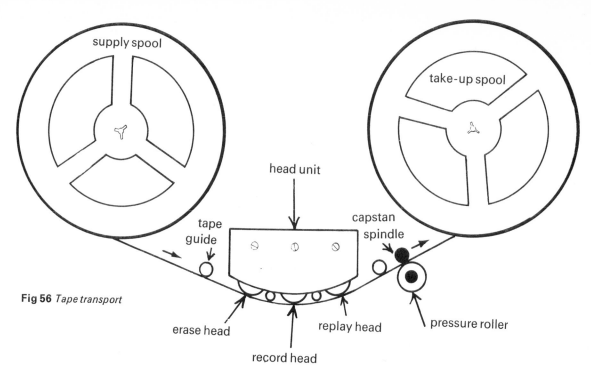

supply spool

take-up spool

head unit

tape guide

capstan spindle

Fig 56 *Tape transport*

erase head

replay head

pressure roller

record head

frequencies are attenuated by comparison with the medium frequencies. The amplifier is provided with an equalizing circuit which compensates for these losses both in recording and playback, so that all frequencies are reproduced as close to the original distribution as possible. Engineers call this a 'flat overall frequency response', and international standards prescribe the degree of equalization in order to ensure that tapes may be recorded on one machine and played back on another.

The amplifier of the electronic section is also operated by means of switches or press buttons. All recorders are equipped with one or more inputs for microphones and most have an additional radio input and a separate input for a pick-up. The radio socket, which is at line level, is often combined for input and output (DIN socket). In this case the input serves for recording the radio programme and the output for the playback of the recorded tapes through the radio set or an external amplifier, or for copying to a second tape recorder. This input allows the copying of records (provided there are no copyright problems) or tape recordings. Some recorders are equipped with separate recording level controls for the different inputs, i.e. with an incorporated mixer.

TAPE SPEEDS Mention.

Most tape recorders offer a choice of speeds selected from 15, $7\frac{1}{2}$, $3\frac{3}{4}$, $1\frac{7}{8}$ and $\frac{15}{16}$ inches per second (38, 19, 9·5, 5 and 2·375 cm/s). Generally, two speeds are provided, for example, $7\frac{1}{2}$ and $3\frac{3}{4}$ i.p.s. though three or even four speeds are available.

Obviously, the slower the tape speed the longer will be the running time. But as a general principle the higher the tape speed the better the quality of the recording. With a slow speed any imperfections in the tape itself become apparent. It is also mechanically more difficult to obtain a perfect speed constancy at a slow rate.

Recording studios normally use 15 i.p.s. In the theatre we have tended to standardize at $7\frac{1}{2}$ i.p.s. The frequency response and dynamic range at this speed is excellent and the amount of tape required held within reasonable limits. It is also a convenient speed for editing. At $3\frac{3}{4}$ i.p.s. cutting in on a bar of music or trying to edit out a 'click' starts to become difficult.

$3\frac{3}{4}$ i.p.s. is useful for long background effects or 'wallpaper' music, and some modern machines produce remarkable results at this speed. At $1\frac{7}{8}$ i.p.s. the loss of high frequencies must be taken into account. Speeds as low as $\frac{15}{16}$ are only really suitable for lengthy dictation or for recording conferences, etc., where the main consideration is a very long uninterrupted recording time.

Tape speed governs frequency range and although there are constant technical developments in both tape and electronics the highest frequencies reproduced by most non-studio quality recorders are approximately as follows:

> 15 i.p.s. up to 25,000 Hz
> $7\frac{1}{2}$ i.p.s. up to 20,000 Hz
> $3\frac{3}{4}$ i.p.s. up to 12,000 Hz
> $1\frac{7}{8}$ i.p.s. up to 8,000 Hz
> $\frac{15}{16}$ i.p.s. up to 4,000 Hz

NUMBER OF TRACKS

The idea of a number of tracks on a tape often causes confusion. First it must be understood that only one side of the tape is coated with an iron oxide solution which is capable of being magnetized. This working side is coated across the whole width and entire length of the tape. The tracks are created by the track configuration of a particular recording head. Thus a full track head with one large single gap will create one track across almost the full width of the tape. A half track head will produce a track nearly half the tape width and a quarter track head will create a track a little less than a quarter of the tape width.

The different number of tracks were developed, just as were the different speeds, as a means of economizing on tape. The half track machine allows you to record on only the top half of the tape; at the end of the tape the reels are interchanged, thus inverting the tape and presenting the unrecorded portion to the top. The tape can then be recorded over the entire length a second time.

Some machines incorporate two quarter track gaps in the record and playback heads which quadruple the playing time of the tape. One is able to record in both directions with the top gap, then repeat the process by switching to the lower gap.

For stereo recording two separate tracks have to be available at the same time. This is achieved by having record and playback heads with either two half-track gaps (upper and lower) or two quarter track gaps. The latter arrangement allows the tape to be used in both directions in stereo.

Naturally, as the two signals being fed to the stereo record head are not identical, a duplicate set of electronics for both record and playback are necessary.

Fig 57 *Track configurations*

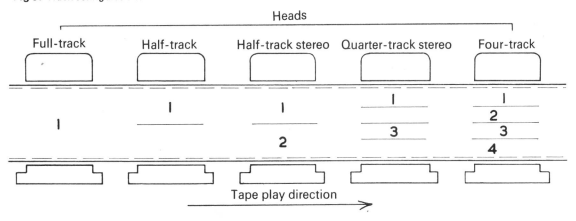

ADVANTAGES AND DISADVANTAGES

Full track Often used in broadcasting and recording studios. Maximum use of the tape provides the best possible dynamic range with little chance of small faults in tape manufacture becoming apparent.

Half track Best compromise providing twice the playing time.

Twin track Two half tracks providing stereo. Most machines have a switch available for cutting out the lower track thereby making the recorder convertible to half track mono.

Quarter track Allows more playing time but with such narrow tracks that particles of dust or imperfections in the tape will be noticeable as a fault in the recording. A minute speck will lift the tape momentarily away from the head, causing a 'drop out' in the reproduced sound. The slower speed of the tape the more likely it is that this will happen. The other drawback of such a narrow track is that it tends to limit the dynamic range the tape will accept.

Quarter track stereo Sometimes misleadingly called 'four track stereo', this provides two stereo signals. The same comments as for quarter track apply.

N.B. When preparing tapes for replay in a performance we need to be able to insert coloured leader tapes as cue markers and, if necessary, we must be able to alter the content of sections of the tape. Therefore we only record in one direction whether it be mono or stereo and whatever the track configuration.

MULTITRACK RECORDING

In order to achieve a number of separate yet synchronous sound tracks, recording studios have developed multitrack tape recorders. Using tape 2 in. (50 mm) wide, up to twenty-four separate tracks can be recorded either all together or one at a time (photograph 26). (There are even thirty-two track machines in existence.) The need for such machines was created by the pop music world where groups record their backing tracks first, adding the voices when the music is to their satisfaction. Having achieved the backing track and first layer of voices, they can then 'track on' the lead singer, more voices, a string section or a symphony orchestra if they can afford it.

There are also machines on the market which provide four tracks on standard $\frac{1}{4}$ in. (6 mm) tape. These can be useful for recording and creating special effects. However, the problems previously mentioned with quarter track stereo recording also apply here.

THE TAPE

The tape used on standard recorders is $\frac{1}{4}$ in. (6 mm) wide and is produced in varying thicknesses. It consists of a plastic-based film coated with particles of iron oxide, which, through various complicated processes, are given a form similar to that of minute needles (i.e. a length of approximately 0·04 thousandths of an inch).

This iron oxide is incorporated into a lacquer which is applied to the base film. The coating process is an extremely critical technique and must produce a layer of constant thickness on the base material. At the same time, the needle-shaped iron oxide particles are magnetically orientated in the lengthwise direction of the tape, which improves the electro-magnetic properties. It is most important that the iron oxide is magnetically stable, ensuring retention of the quality of the recording even after long storage or repeated use.

The coating is then polished, giving the tape a non-abrasive, mirror-smooth surface. This treatment further improves the intimate contact between the tape and the magnetic heads, which in turn improves the high-frequency response. Abrasive effects and drop-out are almost eliminated and wear of the magnetic heads is reduced.

ELECTRO-ACOUSTICAL PROPERTIES

The electro-acoustical properties of a tape cannot be assessed on the basis of the tape alone, because they are influenced by the characteristics of the recorder. Any evaluation, therefore, must be made by comparing the tape to be tested with a standard reference tape. The results obtained, in the same operating conditions, are compared with the known results of the reference tape.

With these factors in mind, we will attempt to explain the most important electro-acoustical properties.

Sensitivity This is the measure of the signal intensity obtained from the tape that has been recorded under specific conditions. A high-sensitivity tape retains a stronger magnetization than a low-sensitivity tape under equal operating conditions and on reproduction will give a higher output voltage. A high-sensitivity tape, therefore, requires less playback amplification, thus giving a better signal-to-noise ratio and greater dynamic range on playback.

Frequency response A frequency response test shows if the tape can reproduce the high and low frequencies equally as well as the middle range. Here also, the value is given in relation to that of the reference tape. Manufacturers line up their tape machines to suit the frequency response characteristics of a particular type of tape and best results will be achieved with the recommended tape.

Harmonic distortion This is the amount of distortion occurring on playback. Extraneous harmonics are produced during the recording process, and these overtones, which were not present in the original signal, are given as a percentage of the total signal. Harmonic distortion increases the more the tape is magnetized and can become objectionable.

PRINT-THROUGH

The adjacent layers of a tape wound on reels have an undesirable tendency to exchange their magnetism and this effect, known as 'print-through', increases with the length of storage time. Today it is possible to produce tapes which have such low print-through that it is barely noticeable.

MODULATION NOISE

This noise signal is caused by irregularities in the coating or impurities and dust on the surface of the tape.

REELS AND SPOOLS

The tape is wound on to a spool and thus becomes a reel of tape. The spools generally range in size from 3 in. (75 mm) in diameter up to 7 in. (175 mm). Some machines will accept a spool size of 8¼ in. (206 mm). Professional tape recorders handle the large 10½ in. (263 mm) spools. Larger spools are available in two types: either with the European 'cine' centre or with the NAB (an American standard spool centre commonly used throughout the world for professional equipment) which requires a large centre hub on the machine.

Ciné

Fig 58 *Spool standards*   N.A.B.

TAPE THICKNESS

Because of its robustness, ease of handling (especially when editing) and its inherent quality standard play tape is used whenever possible in the theatre.

However, a number of thinner tapes have been developed which allow for more tape, and therefore a longer playing time, per reel. These are as follows:

Long play One and a half times the playing time of standard play tape. A good general purpose tape for non-professional work.

Double play Twice the playing time of standard play tape. Particularly suitable for domestic quarter-track machines as the suppleness of the tape allows for maximum contact with the heads. It must be handled with care as it is more easily damaged.

Triple play Treble the playing time of standard play tape. Suitable for recordings of long duration where quality is not critical. Often used on portable machines with small reel sizes. This tape is even more prone to damage.

	Spool Diameter cm/in.		Tape Length m/ft.	
Standard Tape For use with semi-professional and professional machines.	cm	in.	m	ft.
	13	5	180	600
	15	$5\frac{3}{4}$	270	900
	18	7	360	1200
	22	$8\frac{1}{4}$	540	1800
	28	$10\frac{1}{2}$	720	2400
Long Play Tape A general purpose tape of high quality.	8	3	65	210
	10	4	135	450
	11	$4\frac{1}{2}$	180	600
	13	5	270	900
	15	$5\frac{3}{4}$	360	1200
	18	7	540	1800
	22	$8\frac{1}{4}$	810	2700
	28	$10\frac{1}{2}$	1080	3600
Double Play Tape High quality tape with twice the playing time of SP tape. Specially suitable for four track recording.	8	3	90	300
	10	4	180	600
	11	$4\frac{1}{4}$	270	900
	13	5	360	1200
	15	$5\frac{3}{4}$	540	1800
	18	7	730	2400
Triple Play Tape Treble the playing time of standard play tape. Specially suitable for recordings of long duration and for portable machines.	8	3	135	450
	9	$3\frac{1}{2}$	180	600
	10	4	270	900
	11	$4\frac{1}{4}$	360	1200
	13	5	540	1800
	15	$5\frac{3}{4}$	730	2400
	18	7	1080	3600

Which Tape Speed for Which Purpose?

15 i.p.s.
The speed normally used in recording studios for the best dynamic range and frequency response.

$7\frac{1}{2}$ i.p.s.
This speed gives an extended dynamic range and is therefore most suited for Hi-Fi music recordings. In addition, this speed will also facilitate editing.

$3\frac{3}{4}$ i.p.s.
The most popular speed. The frequency response at this speed is excellent and the amount of tape required is kept within a reasonable limit.

$1\frac{7}{8}$ i.p.s.
The loss of high frequencies must be taken into account, although speech can be very satisfactorily recorded at this slow speed.

$\frac{15}{16}$ i.p.s.
A speed as slow as this is only suitable for lengthy dictation or for the recording of conferences, where the main factor is a very long recording time without interruption.

Playing times at a glance

Length m	ft	15 i.p.s. 38 c.p.s.	$7\frac{1}{2}$ i.p.s. 19 c.p.s.	$3\frac{3}{4}$ i.p.s. 9·5 c.p.s.	$1\frac{7}{8}$ i.p.s. 5 c.p.s.	$\frac{15}{16}$ i.p.s. 2·375 c.p.s.
45	150	1·87 min.	3·75 min.	7·5 min.	15 min.	30 min.
65	210	2·75 min.	5·5 min.	11 min.	22 min.	45 min.
90	300	3·75 min.	7·5 min.	15 min.	30 min.	60 min.
135	450	5·5 min.	11 min.	22 min.	45 min.	90 min.
180	600	7·5 min.	15 min.	30 min.	60 min.	120 min.
270	900	11 min.	22 min.	45 min.	90 min.	180 min.
360	1200	15 min.	30 min.	60 min.	120 min.	240 min.
540	1800	22 min.	45 min.	90 min.	180 min.	360 min.
730	2400	30 min.	60 min.	120 min.	240 min.	480 min.
1080	3600	45 min.	90 min.	180 min.	360 min.	720 min.
1280	4200	53·75 min.	107·5 min.	215 min.	430 min.	860 min.

Fig 59 Table of speeds, playing times, types of tape and spool sizes

THE OPERATION

Having chosen our tape, speed and track configuration we now arrive at the stage of making a recording. Let us assume that we are making a monaural recording on a half-track machine at 7½ i.p.s. (19 cm/s) using standard tape. The signal to be recorded is coming via mixer at line level and could therefore originate as one or a number of microphones, tape machines, disc units, etc.

CONNECTION

The mixer is connected to the line input (sometimes labelled 'Radio' 'Auxiliary' or 'Music') of the tape recorder. We have previously ascertained that there is a correct impedance matching and that the interconnecting lead is correctly wired for a balanced or unbalanced system, whichever is applicable. If we were recording with a microphone straight into the machine then it would obviously be plugged into the microphone socket. Here again, impedances and balancing must be watched.

LOUDSPEAKER MONITORING

It is necessary when recording to be able to hear as well as see via the meter what is going on to the tape. A simple way of monitoring is to connect an amplifier and loudspeaker to the mixer. However, with this method one is hearing the original signal before it is recorded. A better method is to connect an amplifier and loudspeaker to the playback head and thus monitor the signal a fraction of a second after it has been recorded. With professional equipment both options are available and simply by flicking a switch one can compare the original with the just-recorded signal.

Most machines are equipped with a monitor headset socket. This will suffice if a loudspeaker is not available. Indeed, a headset is preferable when recording in the same room as the microphone in order to preclude feedback and unwanted echo effects from the playback head.

METER MONITORING

Although an aural quality check is necessary, the recording meter must dictate the input level adjustment, which is made via the Record Gain control.

The rules are very simple: if the signal supplied to the recording head is too low, the playback will have to be amplified to such an extent that all the background noise inherent in both the tape and the recording/playback process will also be amplified. This is described as a poor signal-to-noise ratio. Alternatively, if the signal supplied to the recording head is too high, the result will be an 'overloaded' or badly distorted recording.

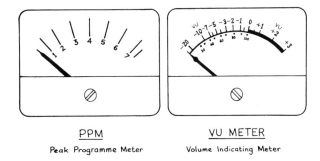

PPM
Peak Programme Meter

VU METER
Volume Indicating Meter

Fig 60 Meters. PPM Peak programme meter: an accurate way of measuring the electrical nature of an audio signal. VU Volume indicating meter: a cheaper device measuring overall loudness, that does not display all the peaks of the electrical signal.

The listening level is adjusted at the playback stage. One should never attempt to make a 'quiet' recording. A correct recording is ensured if the loudest signals, or peaks, are near the maximum level shown on the meter, but it is as well to check the manufacturer's handbook for their recommendations.

N.B. When dubbing from one machine to another it is essential that the machine originating the signal is also set up so that the meter is 'peaking' correctly.

TONE CONTROLS

The tone controls on most tape recorders only affect the playback. Recordings should be made 'flat' and any necessary tone correction or filtering coped with either in the mixer or at the playback stage.

THE RECORDING

1 The tape is on the machine with the full spool on the left and the free end of the tape wound two or three times around the take up reel on the right.

2 The 'coated' side of the tape is facing the magnetic heads.

3 The speed adjustment is set.

4 Any track-selection is set.

5 The tape counter is set at zero. (A note should be made of the material to be recorded with the number on the counter each time the tape is stopped. This provides quick access to any 'take' of a particular recording and will considerably speed up the recording and editing processes.) Be warned that tape counters on different machines will probably not be compatible.

6 The tape machine is in the 'Record' mode. Some machines have to be switched to Record as a safety measure to prevent accidental erasure.

7 The Record Gain is set for optimum level on the meter.

8 Press Record/Play and you are away.

A few hints which might make life easier:
Make it a habit to let the tape continue for several seconds with the Record Gain turned down at the end of each recording. This will make editing easier. It is also particularly important when making a recording on tape which has already been used, as it will erase any existing material and provide you with a quiet pause.

At the beginning of each recording start the machine and leave a few seconds before cueing in and fading up the signal to be recorded. This allows the tape to attain an even speed and keeps any clicks or noises from the starting action well clear of programme material. This also helps editing. Always preface each recorded item with a verbal identification (e.g., Cue 6 – Take 3) and keep a corresponding list.

Label and keep careful records of all recorded material.

Keep a close check during recording that the levels are neither too low nor too high and make gentle adjustments as necessary.

All fading in and out at beginnings and ends of cues must be done slowly and smoothly. The background noise of a recording, whether the actual room acoustic or noise from the tape itself, becomes much more apparent if it comes in or breaks off abruptly.

When recording with a microphone in remote locations, it is a good idea to record a stretch of room acoustic on its own without altering the record level set up for the session. This can be useful for splicing-in pauses which might become necessary at a later date.

Handle the tapes as little as possible. Grease from fingers attracts dirt.

Keep tapes well clear of magnetic equipment (transformers, magnets, ribbon and dynamic microphones, etc.).

MICROPHONE RECORDING TECHNIQUE

This is the most difficult of all recording operations since so many external influences can affect the result. First make sure that the microphone is so placed that it will not pick up any mechanical sounds from the tape recorder itself. Ideally, the microphone should be in an acoustically treated room separated and soundproofed from all the recording equipment, i.e. a recording studio. If this is not possible then a quiet room with the minimum of external noises should be found. The room should have as little reverberation as possible. If there are curtains they should be drawn to help shut out external noise and deaden reflected sounds within the room itself. Carpets also have a good deadening effect. If such a room is not available it should be possible to rig up a tent or some screens covered in heavy material to surround the microphone on three sides.

In a situation which is acoustically too live it is obviously preferable to use a directional microphone rather than an omnidirectional which will pick up reflected sounds from all angles.

The microphone should be placed at a suitable distance from the sound source. A distance of one foot (300 mm) is ideal for most speech conditions, although some quiet speakers might need to be as close as five or six inches (125–150 mm). With such close techniques there is a danger of breath noise or 'popping' which is an explosive effect on the diaphragm. This can be remedied either by placing the microphone slightly off axis to the speaker or by using a wind-shield (or pop-gag). This is either a sock or a small cage containing foam rubber or some similar substance which absorbs the shock waves of air. As the name implies they are also used for outside recording to minimize wind effects. The only drawback with a wind-shield is that it slightly impedes the higher frequencies.

If the speaker is too far from the microphone the 'body' of the voice is lost by an apparent diminishing in bass response, and the ratio of the direct sound to its reflections becomes poor. If you wish to achieve a distant effect, use a reasonably close-microphone technique but keep to the dead side of the microphone.

For stereophonic recording most engineers use a pair of crossed directional microphones. For larger recording sessions (particularly in orchestral broadcasting) additional 'fill-in' microphones may be placed to highlight certain sections. These are then added to one or other of the stereo channels via a mixer. Two separate microphones may, of course, be used, but the farther apart they are the wider the acoustic separation becomes. The result is a 'hole' in the middle of the stereo image. In fact, the recording becomes two-track and is no longer true stereo.

Fig 61 *Temporary recording tent*

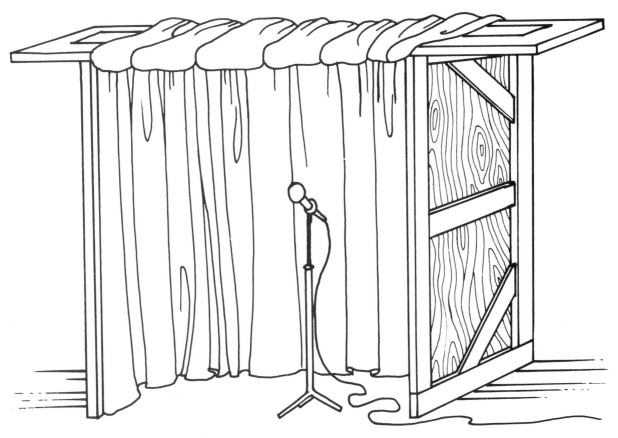

Fig 62 *Windshield or pop gag*

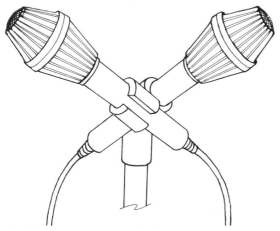

Fig 63 *Crossed stereo pair of microphones*

In recording studios stereo is created artificially within the mixing desk. Each instrument is separately miked, the recording (mixing) engineer being responsible for balancing the sound. Each microphone is then routed via a 'pan' control to stereo left, stereo right or anywhere in between. In this way the engineer has complete control over his stereo picture. A similar technique was used in the theatre for the London production of *Jesus Christ Superstar* which we shall be discussing later.

FAULTS AND MAINTENANCE

Sometimes results do not quite measure up to expectations. If the quality of the reproduction does not seem to be as good as it could be, the cause is not always a defective recorder or recording tape : it can be the fault of the opera-

tor. Silly things can happen, like under or over-recording, placing the tape on the machine with the oxide away from the recording heads, selecting the wrong tape speed or overlooking a faulty connection.

Dust and dirt can also cause trouble with both the tape and the machine. To avoid the possibility of drop-outs caused by dirt tapes should always be stored in their boxes.

No reproduction Tape incorrectly threaded. Faulty connection to monitor amplifier/loudspeaker. Internal loudspeaker switched off. Wrong track selected. Machine not in correct playback mode.

Inadequate erasing One of the main causes is a faulty alignment of the magnetic heads, i.e. the erasing track does not fully cover the recording track. (This may also be the reason for unsatisfactory reproduction.) It could also be caused by faulty tape-guides, insufficient contact between the tape and the erasing head, a weak and defective oscillator, or an open or short-circuited erase head.

Two tracks blend into each other (*cross talk*) This results from incorrect positioning of the heads or faulty tape-guides which cause the tape to move up and down when passing the heads.

Damaged tapes may be the result of too high a tape tension, faulty brakes, badly aligned or dirty tape guides.

Wow and flutter These objectionable variations in sound pitch are an audible sign of malfunction in the tape transport mechanism. They are most commonly caused by : build up of dirt on the capstan, inadequate pressure of the pinch roller, too high clutch friction of the supply reel shaft or a faulty clutch on the other spooling.

Chirping and squealing sounds These are caused by tape vibrations resulting from defective pressure pads or from an accumulation of dust or dirt. The felt pads should be cleaned or replaced. Finally, it is also advisable to clean the different parts of the tape guides.

Excessive head wear This can occur if the tape tension is excessively high. Poor quality tapes have an abrasive surface which is also conducive to head wear. Worn heads will affect the frequency response. Defective tape lifters also lead to head wear when fast spooling.

Fig 64 *Crossed pair with fill ins*

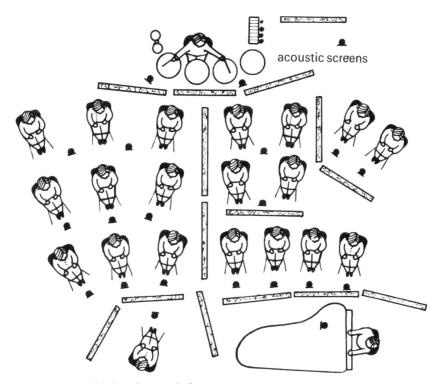

acoustic screens

Fig 65 *Artificial stereo with multimicrophone technique.*
Each microphone is 'panned' as required at the mixing
desk.

Tape spillage or poor take-up Bad spooling of the tape on the take-up reel may be caused by incorrect adjustment of either the clutches or the brakes. Tape spillage usually results from incorrect synchronization between take-up and supply reel brakes. Under these conditions, the supply reel continues to feed tape after the take-up reel has stopped. As a temporary measure to avoid tape spillage, the tape may be kept taut by using the hand as a brake on the supply reel.

Erratic response This is also caused by incorrect tape tension. Inadequate tension results in the loss of intimate contact between the tape and the heads.

Poor high-frequency response A severe loss of high frequencies is most often caused by a worn head, in which the metal of the pole-piece has worn away, enlarging the head gap. Worn heads must be replaced. If this loss becomes apparent only with old recordings, or with those made on different recorders, it may be because the vertical alignment of the head gap (azimuth) is faulty.

Maintenance The capstan, pinch wheel, tape guides and all three heads must be examined at regular intervals for the accumulation of oxide dust. Any coating should be wiped off with a soft piece of cloth slightly moistened with methylated spirits or alcohol.
CAUTION Never use carbon tetrachloride, which even in small quantities will ruin the tape base or cause slippage in the friction drive mechanism. Also remember that these parts should never be scraped with any metallic or hard objects. If you have inadvertently placed a magnetized screw-driver or some other tool on the heads or tape guides they must be demagnetized. Demagnetizers can be purchased from most dealers in electronic equipment, and should be used every once in a while to 'demag' the heads.

EDITING

When preparing a tape for a show the editing is as important as the recording. It is a very simple process and once the basic rules are known the skill can be developed only with a great deal of practice. Editing performs various functions:

1 Removing unwanted 'takes'.
2 Removing clicks or other noises.
3 Placing all the cues in their correct order.
4 Cleaning up the beginning and end of each cue.
5 Splicing coloured marker tapes between each cue.
6 Building up sound montage effects by splicing together various preselected sounds.
7 Timing: shortening cues by cutting out sections or lengthening them by insertions or additions.
8 Inserting a metallic strip or section of translucent tape before the start of each cue when the tape is to be used with a machine incorporating an automatic stopping device.

EDITING KIT

There are many different types of editing equipment and proprietary splicing gadgets designed to catch the eye in hi-fi shops, but professionals pretty well unanimously go for the same simple kit:

One splicing block.

One packet of single-edged razor blades.

One pair of unmagnetized scissors. Special brass editing scissors are strongly recommended. Alternatively, a head demagnetizer should be used to ensure that the scissors and razor blade do not become 'magged up'. Cutting with a magnetized instrument will affect the tape and cause a click.

One reel of splicing tape 7/32 in. (approx. 5 mm) wide. It is very important to use this width which is a little less than the $\frac{1}{4}$ in. (6 mm) tape. Do not be talked into buying the $\frac{1}{2}$ in. (13 mm) variety.

Several reels of coloured leader tape. Choose a make which has a matt side suitable for writing on with a ball-point pen.

One white chinagraph pencil

One stopwatch

Several empty spools

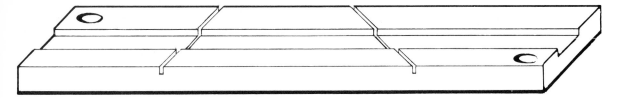

Fig 66 *Splicing block. Emitape block in the UK (EMI Ltd). Editall tape splicer in the USA (Tech. Labs. Inc.).*

In addition to these items you also require a cue sheet giving full details of the order and timings required for the final tape or tapes, and a recording sheet listing everything from the recording sessions.

The first vital step is to make absolutely sure that you know which is the playback head. Unless you have a non-standard machine it will be the one on the right nearest the capstan.

Once you are ready to edit find the beginning of the first cue by playing the machine and pressing the stop button as soon as you hear it. Then locate the exact point by moving the tape smoothly backwards and forwards over the heads, turning the reels by hand. (Practise this a lot, being careful not to stretch the tape.)

When you are sure that the sound is actually at the gap on the replay head, make a small mark with the chinagraph pencil. Do this carefully, to avoid damaging the head. You can then rewind the tape a few inches and run it at normal speed, checking that the mark coincides with the sound. Another method is to put the machine into the Play mode with the pause control held, and to move the tape until the mark centres on the head. When the pause control is released, the sound should start immediately.

Once satisfied that the mark is correct, cut the tape about half an inch (13 mm) away from the mark. CAUTION Always cut on the opposite side of the head to the wanted sound; i.e. if it is the start of a cue, cut on the right of the head, and if it is the end of a cue cut on the left.

Take the wanted end of the tape and place it in the splicing block with the mark at the centre of the 45 degree cutting guide. The 90 degree guide is only used for really critical editing as the join is not so strong and the result may be a click or thump as the tape goes past the heads.

Now cut off a sufficient length of leader tape and place one end overlapping the cutting guide by about an inch (25 mm).

Holding the razor blade firmly at an angle of slightly less than 45 degrees, place the point in the cutting guide and slice the tape gently but firmly across.

There should now be two ends neatly butted together with a small end of waste on top which can be removed with a fingernail or the point of the razor blade.

The final step is to cut off about an inch (25 mm) of the self-adhesive splicing tape and lay it very carefully along the groove over the two pieces of tape, making sure that it does not overlap at the edges. Any overlap can cause the tape to snag and break; it can also contaminate the heads with adhesive material. If you are satisfied with the lay of the splicing tape, press it into position and remove all air-bubbles by rubbing it firmly either with a finger or thumb nail or the rounded handle of the scissors. Having checked that the two pieces of tape still butt and do not overlap, the job is done.

A few hints

1 Always edit the start of cues close to the leader to facilitate quick and accurate cueing-in during a performance.

2 Always leave a little spare tape at the end of each cue to allow for wastage in the event of having to re-edit.

3 When re-editing always leave the leader into the cue intact and pull apart the end of the cue where a split end or a tear will not matter.

4 Use light-coloured marker tape between cues for easy identification under poor lighting conditions.

5 Coloured marker tapes should have the matt side away from the heads so that a cue-number or other written identification can be seen during playback.

6 It is a good idea to insert a completely different coloured marker every so often for quick identification when fast spooling during rehearsals. I would suggest not only between every act and every scene, but also at the end of any particular sequence of cues.

7 Make a 'protection copy' of your final tape in case of disasters.

AUTOMATIC STOPS

Machines incorporating an automatic stopping mechanism are recommended for theatre installations especially where two or more machines might be in operation at the same time. The operator can then concentrate on cueing in his tapes and obtaining the correct sound balance.

The two main ways of effecting an automatic stop are *a*) with a metallic strip fixed to the tape which hits two electrical contacts placed near the heads, thus completing a switching circuit, and *b*) by means of a photo electric cell on one side of the tape and a small light on the other which, as soon as the tape runs out or there is a translucent section, allows the light to shine on the cell and completes a switch circuit.

The first method simply requires an inch (25 mm) of self-adhesive metal foil (Scotch 51) stuck to the inside of the leader tape in a suitable place to stop the machine as close as possible to the next start position.

For the photo electric cell one can either splice in a short strip of clear leader tape, or remove an inch of coating from the coloured tape itself. This can be done by scraping carefully with a razor blade or, better still, by wiping it off with a cloth moistened with acetone.

CARTRIDGE MACHINES

These machines were developed particularly for use on radio stations for the convenient handling of jingles and commercials, and because they are so easy to handle, they are sometimes used in the theatre, although a separate cartridge is needed for each effect.

The $\frac{1}{4}$ in. (6 mm) tape is contained on a single spool within an enclosed plastic cartridge with the tape exposed at the front like a standard cassette. The spool is actually a turntable with a centre hub around which the tape is wound with the loose end at the centre brought off, threaded round guides and joined to the other end. This creates a contained endless loop. The cartridge slots into a letter box opening in the machine which operates like a normal tape recorder except that the playing time is limited by the length of the tape loop.

The machines are so designed that at the start of each recording a pulse is automatically placed on the tape which, under playback conditions, triggers a relay to stop the machine. Thus if the sound effect runs for thirty seconds but the duration of the tape loop is one minute the machine will continue for the thirty seconds of blank tape. It will then stop with the start of the effect ready to go again.

Cartridges are very compact, mechanically silent and extremely accurate in operation. But there are drawbacks. For example, it is not possible to perform the speedy edits that are often required during rehearsals; one always has to go back to the original conventional tape master for editing purposes and then transfer back to the cartridge. And there are no rapid spooling facilities. With some machines it is possible to run forwards at double speed, but this can mean a wait of half the playing time of the entire cartridge in order to set back (or rather forward) to the beginning. Under strained rehearsal conditions this can be a serious drawback. This lack of spooling ability is also inconvenient with cues of indeterminate length where with a conventional tape machine one can fade out at any point and quickly spool on to the next leader.

Despite these disadvantages I feel that as cartridge machines develop they will increasingly be used in theatre control rooms, perhaps eventually replacing reel to reel machines altogether.

1 *Portable public address system with mixer/amplifier
and loudspeakers.* Photo Courtesy Shure Electronics Ltd

2 *Portable theatre system*

3 *Cut-away section of a dual concentric loudspeaker. The tweeter is the centre portion of the cone and the separate bass and treble drivers are incorporated in the same mounting.* Photo Courtesy Tannoy

4 *The five bass bins and horns installed behind the cinema screen at the Queen Elizabeth Hall, London.*
Photo Courtesy Vitavox

5 *Stereo amplifier capable of producing 60 watts continuous programme output per channel. By making a small adjustment inside, it can become a single 100 watt amplifier.* Photo Courtesy McInnes Laboratories

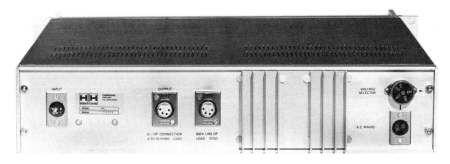

6 *Rear of a mono power amplifier showing the line input jack socket, the loudspeaker terminal connections for 8 ohms or 16 ohms, plus an alternative 100 volt line output.* Photo Courtesy H/H Electronics Ltd

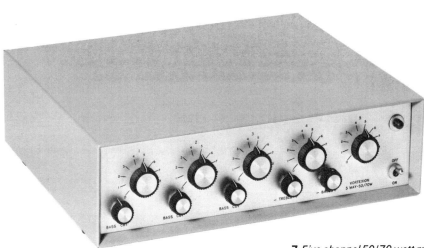

7 *Five channel 50/70 watt mixer/amplifier.* Photo Courtesy Vortexion Ltd

8 *Mono mixer incorporating four microphone inputs and one auxiliary or line input, plus overall master control.*
Photo Courtesy Shure Electronics Ltd

9 *A quasi-stereo mixer with three microphone inputs switchable left or right, one microphone input with pan from left to right, and an auxiliary or line input with separate concentric gain controls for left and right.*
Photo Courtesy Shure Electronics Ltd

1	Input	11	Left Master	21	Left Output
2	Equalization	12	Right Master	22	Foldback Output
3	Foldback	13	Headphone Output	23	Echo Input 2
4	Echo	14	Monitor Volume	24	Echo Input 1
5	Stereo Pan	15	Monitor Select Switch	25	Echo Output
6	Channel On/Off Monitor Selector	16	Meter Selecter Switch	26	Multicore Connector for Inputs/Outputs
7	Fader	17	VU Meters	27	Microphone Inputs: 200 OHM Balanced
8	Aluminium Flight Case with Lid	18	Mains Input		
9	Echo Master	19	Voltage Tap Changer and Fuse		
10	Foldback Master	20	Right Output		

10 *Sixteen-channel stereo mixing desk designed for touring.* Photo Courtesy Soundcraft Electronics Ltd

11 *Typical input channel facilities for stereo mixing desk.*
Photo Courtesy Alice (Stancoil) Ltd

12 *A custom built mixing desk for a recording studio with 32 inputs and 24 output groups plus the complicated foldback and monitoring facilities necessary for multitrack recording.* Photo Courtesy Rupert Neve and Company Ltd

13 *Example of a theatre sound control room with a six input four output mixing desk with loudspeaker routing on the right. Extra microphone inputs come via small sub-mixer. Note the large opening window, the recessed and lit plug panel, the two remotely controlled tape machines and the sunken turntable unit with flush perspex lid. Mixer: Electrosonic Ltd.* Photo Courtesy Theatre Projects Consultants Ltd

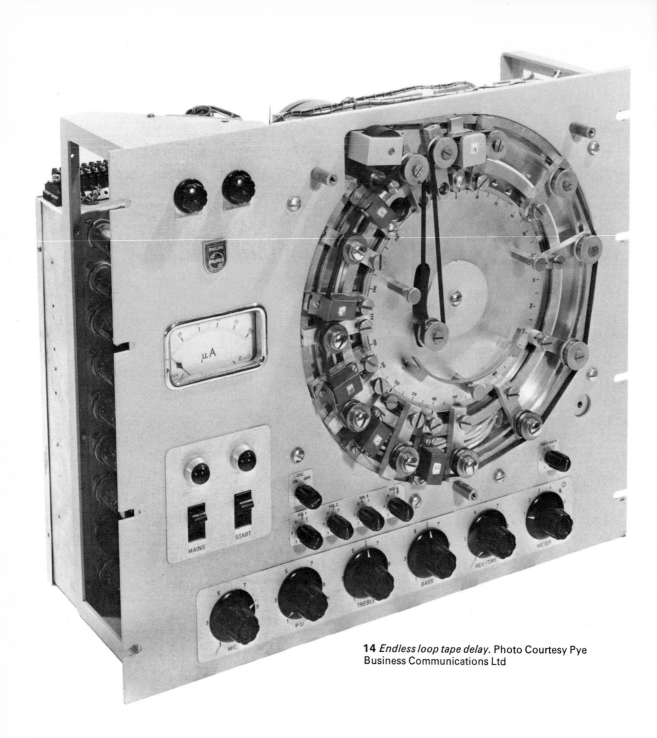

14 *Endless loop tape delay.* Photo Courtesy Pye Business Communications Ltd

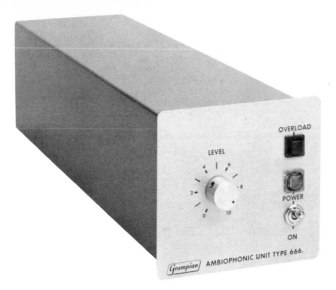

15 *Echo spring.* Photo Courtesy Grampian Reproducers Ltd

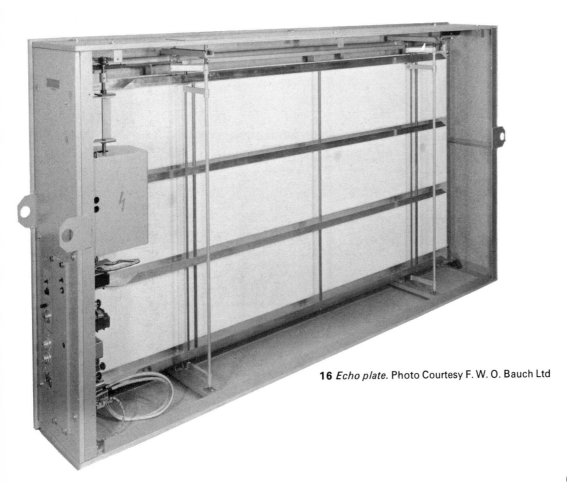

16 *Echo plate.* Photo Courtesy F. W. O. Bauch Ltd

17 *Four speed transcription turntable with an infinitely variable speed control which can be very useful for sound effects.* Photo Courtesy Goldring Ltd

19 *High quality pick-up arm with accurate weight adjustment.* Photo Courtesy S.M.E. Ltd

18 *Turntable unit with preamplifier.* Photo Courtesy Sinclair Ltd

20 *Examples of typical microphones*

a *Shure 545D cardioid dynamic*

b *Shure 565SD cardioid dynamic*

d *AKG D224C cardioid dynamic*

c *Altec 651AH cardioid dynamic*

e *AKG C12A variable pattern condenser*

f *Neumann UHIT* variable pattern condenser

g *Sennheiser MD211 omnidirectional dynamic*

h *Beyer M88 hypercardioid dynamic*

i *STC 4038 bidirectional ribbon*

21 *Locating the cue by hand*

22 *Marking the tape*

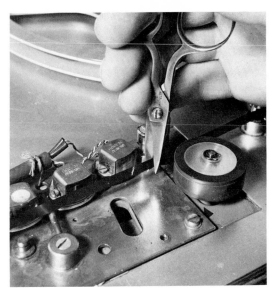

23 *Snipping the tape to the waste side of the mark*

24 *Cutting in the block the two ends of tape to be joined*

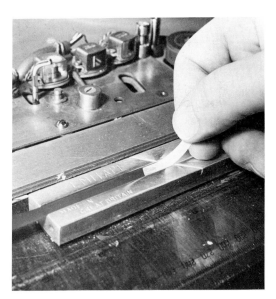

25 *Positioning the splicing tape*

26 *Twenty-four-track studio tape recorder.* Photo Courtesy F. W. O. Bauch Ltd

10 The control position

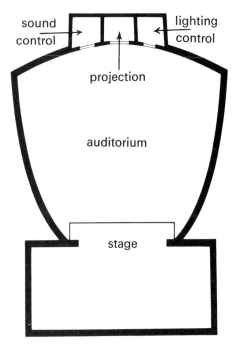

Fig 67 *Typical control room positions*

It is as important for the sound technician to hear what the audience is hearing as for the lighting switchboard operator to see what the audience is seeing. It can even be argued that with a complicated sound balance it is much more important. For whereas lighting levels when plotted will remain the same for every performance, sound levels will vary. The number of people in the auditorium, even the clothes they are wearing (whether lightweight or heavy and absorbent) will have an influence. The amount of humidity in the air also has an effect. When one is working with microphones the changes can be quite dramatic. Every performance will need a slightly different balance. A particular artiste may be 'giving' more or less or he may be at a different distance from the microphone; or the orchestra may be playing louder or softer, and so on.

It is therefore of the utmost importance that a permanent sound control position is centrally placed within the auditorium. Ideally, it should be a room at the centre rear of the stalls or circle. (The central position is particularly vital for balancing stereo.) It should be sound proofed to the auditorium but have a very large window, which opens easily and quietly, with an unrestricted view of the stage and orchestra pit.

The mixing desk should either be very narrow back to front or be placed sideways on to the window. This will allow the operator to listen close to the auditorium and not be confused by the acoustics of the room in which he is sitting.

Monitor loudspeakers should be provided for recording, editing, lining up and checking cues, etc. Under live performance conditions, however, these monitors can be no substitute for listening to the real thing. We are dealing not only with a balance between loudness and softness, live action and electronic sound, but a balance between many widely spaced loudspeakers. Unlike a recording studio or radio station we are working in three dimensions. And there is the added complication of always bearing in mind the differences in perspective from various seating positions within the auditorium, i.e. the front row of the stalls and the back row of the balcony.

The control room should have space for the mixing desk, one or two turntables, two or more tape machines and a certain amount of storage. There should also be adequate silent ventilation.

Being the nerve centre of the sound system, all permanent wiring will terminate here. It is recommended that high level and low level lines be brought to separate plug panels. This is a flexible arrangement which also allows broadcasting or recording organizations to share the facilities.

There should be a single phase main supply complete with a mains switch and indicator lamp. A generous supply of standard 13 amp (15 amp in US) 3-pin sockets should provide for all permanent installations as well as any extra equipment which may be required. It is essential to have a good earth (ground).

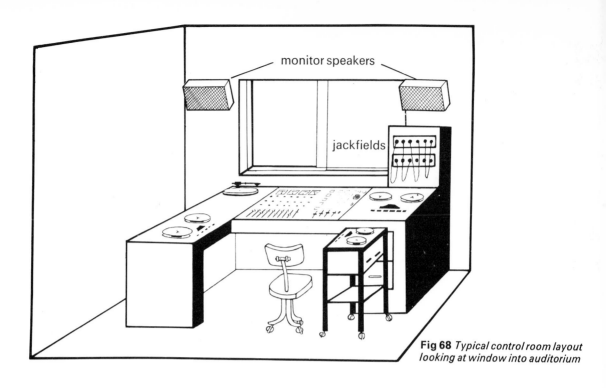

Fig 68 *Typical control room layout looking at window into auditorium*

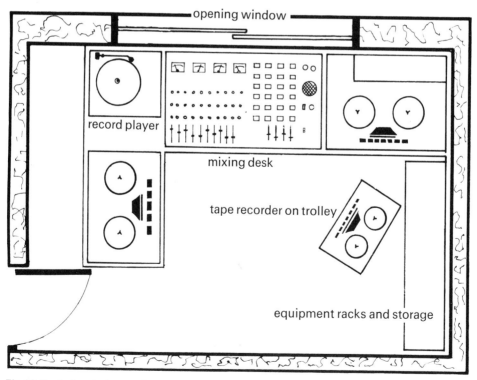

Fig 69 *Typical control room plan*

PART 2

11 Sound effects

THEIR USE AND CREATION

In the 1950s when I first became involved with theatre sound, as a stage manager at that time, the use of 78 r.p.m. sound effects discs was still prevalent. The sounds were selected from the fairly basic libraries that were available and then transferred to disc. Usually only two or three items were recorded on each single-side to allow for maximum flexibility during mixing. Music was still obtainable on 78 r.p.m. commercial discs since the new long playing record (at that incredibly slow speed of $33\frac{1}{3}$ r.p.m.) was only just being introduced.

The turntable units were rugged affairs, incorporating large valve amplifiers and loudspeaker switching. Each pick-up arm had a lowering device and some form of patent groove-locator. In the UK, these large gramophones were called 'panatropes' and even today some of the more established stage managers still write 'Pan cues' in their prompt scripts (photographs 27 and 28).

As an assistant stage manager I have worked with six turntables and upwards of thirty discs, all boldly numbered for quick reference. This method of working was very convenient during rehearsals because it allowed the director to call for any combination, sequence and balance of effects. Everything then depended on the skill of the operator. It is interesting to note that the BBC and other broadcasting authorities, with their fast turnover of programmes, still use sound effects discs for the same reasons.

In 1957, during the last scene of *Brouhaha* at the Aldwych Theatre in London, Peter Sellers, playing the Sultan of an impoverished Arab country, stood alone on stage shouting directions at a number of foreign ships which were supposed to be arriving through the auditorium bringing his people aid. Each instruction was followed by a sound effect of, say, a ship's siren, two ships colliding, men shouting, a ship going aground, a ship sinking, etc. During one short page of script there were twenty or more

sound cues using four turntables and a large collection of discs. An added complication was that Mr Sellers, who is not actually known for keeping to the script, on more than one occasion deliberately gave the wrong line – paused – listened – then gleefully pronounced 'Aha, that caught you out!', knowing that off stage confusion reigned with discs flying in all directions. We eventually learned to cope with this situation by filling in with strange strangulated noises into a microphone while hurriedly rearranging the turntables.

Soon after this era of the panatrope it became the practice to rehearse and open a show using discs. Once the show was set and looked likely to run, it was all transferred to tape, which was easier, more accurate to operate and, even more important, more durable. Lacquer discs had to be renewed about every four weeks in order to maintain a reasonably scratch-free quality.

This transitional stage lasted some eight to ten years. At the beginning of the 1960s tape was firmly established in London's West End theatres and disc was only used for playing the National Anthem and scene-change music in those theatres already possessing a panatrope.

THE USE OF SOUND

Sound effects may be used for a variety of reasons:

1 To establish (*a*) locale (*b*) time of year (*c*) day or night (*d*) weather conditions

2 To evoke atmosphere

3 To link scenes

4 As an emotional stimulus

5 To reproduce physical happenings: spot cues like cars arriving, babies crying, clocks striking, elephants falling out of trees, etc.

Background effects Let us take background and atmospheric sounds first. Just pause for a moment and listen. . . . I guarantee you are now aware of a whole spectrum of background noises of which you were not fully conscious a moment ago. These are the reassuring and comfortable sounds of life, of people, of things going on.

I am not, however, advocating a continual racket of birds, bells, traffic, radios, etc., running throughout the play. Far from it. Much thought must go into a good background sound track which should, as in real life, register for the most part only on a subconscious level.

In the theatre we have the tremendous advantage of being able to add to and subtract from the background at will; at one moment strengthening a dramatic pause, at another adding to a confusion, thereby giving depth, life and atmosphere to the whole.

A sudden silence or absence of sound can be equally disturbing as a sudden loud noise. This artifice was used to great effect by Peter Hall in his original London production of *Cat on a Hot Tin Roof*. The hot still atmosphere of the deep South was created by using a combination of continuously cheeping crickets and various croaking frog noises with occasionally, during a pause, the harsh squawk of a bird.

The method was, for example, to start a scene with a cricket chirping slowly and repetitively out on the verandah, then when the action was under way very subtly to add some deeper frog noises; a couple of pages later these would be supplemented by the high pitched and continuous sound of cicadas. Having built up the background over quite a long period in order to achieve total acceptance by the audience, dramatic moments could be heightened by merely subtracting one or more of the elements. At one moment I had two types of cricket and three different frog sounds all going at once until, in the middle of the last line of a tense exchange, they all abruptly disappeared. The ensuing pause was electric.

Although there must have been well over seventy sound cues in that production, including plantation workers singing, a distant church bell, an offstage party, children shouting and several radio sequences, many friends who saw the show were unable to remember sound effects at all. That kind of total integration of effects in a production is the essence of a good sound track.

One of the real cliché effects for creating tension is the heartbeat, and under the right circumstances it really does work. We have noticed even in our own sound effects department that when working with music or effects which have a slow rhythmic beat everyone tends to work more slowly than if the beat is fast. The pulse rate changes. This phenomenon can be applied to an audience.

In a production of *Macbeth* I once used a very low frequency drumbeat during the scenes leading up to the battle. It started at a little below the speed of a normal heartbeat and was played at a very low level, with the gain being increased imperceptibly over a long period during which the speed of the beat was also gradually increased, the idea being that it would carry the audiences' pulse rates with it. During some final frenzied activity on stage a few moments before the start of the battle the drumbeat which was by now quite loud and fast was suddenly cut. There was a pause . . . the audience were on the edges of their seats . . . then crash! trumpets, shouting, swords clashing and all hell let loose.

This sequence used the increasing heartbeat effect, the heightened pause and the shock of a sudden loud sound.

It often happens that a continuous background sound creates a distraction. This is especially true in a large theatre where intelligibility is a problem. In all too many places of entertainment one has difficulty in hearing the proceedings because of the hum of an air-conditioning plant or the rumble of traffic. Because this low frequency sound is constant it tends to be discounted, but the effect is of an aural barrier between the actors and the audience.

To run a wind or rain effect, for example, throughout an entire twenty minute scene at a fixed volume level is seldom a good idea. Maybe it is supposed to be raining but it is not necessary to hear it all the time. When it rains in real life we hear it usually when it starts (change of background) and then only become aware of it spasmodically, particularly during pauses in concentration.

In a theatrical situation the rain would either be brought in suddenly to denote a downpour or would be faded in under dialogue some thirty seconds before it was actually required in context. The audience should register the fact that it is raining and then turn their concentration back to the action (if they do not, then we are all in trouble). The level can now be adjusted so that the effect is gently lost under the scene. In other words, we are assisting the concentration process and moving the focus back to the actors. The rain should then occasionally be brought back to be registered during pauses. The reasons for bringing it back are as follows:

1 Because the text calls for it.

2 Because the director wishes to remind the audience of the world outside.

3 Because the scene requires punctuation.

An obvious place to bring back an effect is when someone enters or leaves the stage setting; not only does this action relate to the world outside but it is usually a punctuation point in the scene.

A sensitive use of background sound can add an interesting and important dimension to the setting.

Spot effects Specific spot effects can also do a great deal to help atmosphere. They should, however, be used sparingly and always to some purpose (the aforementioned three reasons). They should be cued-in accurately at every performance just as a film sound editor will precisely position his various voice, music and effects tracks. Good spot effects can assist the actor by giving him another element against which he can react. For example, a scene with a period setting inside a house: at a suitable moment the distant sound of a horse and carriage or a street seller shouting his wares is heard. The actor, without necessarily even pausing, gives the merest glance towards the window and the reality of the situation is immediately enhanced.

Commercial recordings Most of the everyday sounds of weather, traffic, birds, animals, aircraft, bells, people, etc. can be obtained on commercial recordings. However, these recordings are limited both in the range of available sounds and in the duration of the tracks. They are aimed primarily at the amateur movie maker who seldom requires lengthy effects.

Tape loops It is possible to lengthen an effect by recording it on to tape and making a continuous tape loop of it by splicing the beginning of the sound on to the end. The loop is then placed on to a tape machine, ensuring that sufficient ten-

sion is maintained by running it round some smooth heavy object (such as a microphone stand), played back and recorded on to a second tape machine. It is hazardous to use tape loops during a performance.

To avoid an unpleasant hiccoughing effect it is essential to ensure at the beginning and end of the loop that both the content of the sound and the recording levels are identical.

Short loops are seldom satisfactory because their repetitive pattern makes them recognizable as such. This can, however, sometimes be used to advantage: a slow tolling bell, for example, can be made to ring rapidly by making up a loop of a single strike to the length required. If the dying away reverberation is required to complete the effect, then the last note from the original is recorded and spliced on to the end. Other rhythmic sounds of machinery, drumbeats, ghostly breathing, footsteps, etc., can be created in this manner.

It is also worth experimenting with playing loops backwards. For example, a cymbal crash beginning with the reverberation, building up to the initial percussion then cutting back to the reverberation can form the basis of an interesting effect.

With a very lengthy background effect even a long loop can become repetitive. The answer here is to make up two identical loops and play them back out of sync. on two tape machines. After recording the first loop for a while 'cross-fade' to the second to break up the rhythm. N.B. When cross-fading always establish the sound you are bringing in before losing the original. Do it by listening and checking the meter and not by watching the positions of the faders. The object is to avoid a dip or hole in the programme.

Location recording Given a portable tape recorder of sufficient quality many natural sounds can be captured. But, be warned, this is not as easy as it would appear. Let us take a few examples:

1 *Birds in the wild* First find your bird, then get near enough to make a recording, then persuade it to sing.

2 *Animals in the wild* The same applies but can be more dangerous!

3 *Surf breaking* On an open beach if there are not people or birds in the background then

77

there will probably be a wind to upset the microphone. (A windshield is a must for most outside recording.) Surf recorded too near is unnatural because only one wave appears to be breaking, but when recorded at too great a distance it sounds like hiss and extraneous noises are difficult to avoid.

4 *Wind* The main problem with wind is that one has to be sheltered from it in order to be able to record it. Light winds are almost impossible as they hardly register on the meter, therefore the signal-to-noise ratio is bad. When a light wind is played back and amplified in a theatre it is not usually recognizable as such. A strong wind often creates unwanted side effects like rattling shutters, singing telegraph wires, etc.

5 *Traffic* It is difficult to find good town traffic free from the other sounds associated with urban life.

6 *Aeroplanes* Get near enough then stop all the birds and traffic in the vicinity.

7 *Vehicles* It is relatively easy to record a car or motorcycle, assuming you find a deserted place in the dead of night. The difficulty comes in the unending combinations of starting – running – stopping – stalling – reversing, fast – medium – slow, well – badly, interior – exterior, road surface – gravel surface, large engine – small engine, sports – saloon, ancient – modern, doors – horns.

8 *Church bells* The problems of recording church bells and clocks are very basic: outside the church there are too many extraneous noises, and inside the church the sounds of the ringing mechanism are discernible.

Despite what I have just said location recording of effects can be both fun and rewarding. The requirements are a good battery operated tape recorder with a pair of headphones, a directional microphone with an efficient windshield and patience. It is a matter of personal preference but some people use an ordinary cardioid, some a hypercardioid or rifle and others insist that the best results are obtained by means of a parabolic reflector (photograph 32). This is merely a metal dish, or parabola, which collects sounds (rather like cupping your hands behind your ears). The microphone is fixed to a clamp in the centre of the dish and points into the dish. One of the drawbacks of the reflector is that unless one has an enormously large dish made of the right type of material only the high frequencies are collected. Hence the extensive use of parabolas for bird recording.

Simulated effects Certain sounds can be successfully simulated in front of a microphone with the added advantage that extraneous noises can be eliminated completely. Here are a few suggestions:

Rain Method one: take 15–20 dried peas and let them roll back and forth over a fine-meshed wire sieve directly above the microphone.
Method two: make a chute about 12 inches (300 mm) long of grease-proof paper, place the microphone underneath and pour down a constant trickle of castor (grain) sugar.

Wind Pull a length of silk across two or three wooden boards. The strength of the wind can be increased or decreased by varying the amount of drag. For wind in the trees agitate a handful of old recording tape in front of the microphone.

Thunder This can be achieved by breathing gently on the microphone; preferably not an expensive ribbon microphone.

Artillery fire Method one: a short percussive breath on the microphone.
Method two: burst a paper bag while recording at 15 i.p.s. (38 cm/s) and play it back at $3\frac{3}{4}$ i.p.s. (9·5 cm/s).

Waves Take two brushes and move them in opposite directions across a long sheet of metal.

Water lapping Agitate the surface of some water in a plastic bucket and record the sound of the water lapping against the sides.

Rowing boat Dip a piece of wood rhythmically into the water and make a rusty hinge or door squeak in unison.

Fire Crush cellophane paper in front of the microphone. A matchbox being crushed will add another dimension. A pan of sizzling fat is also effective.

Ship's siren Blow across the neck of a bottle half filled with water; the less water in the bottle the deeper the sound.

Comic steam train Take two wooden blocks

covered with sandpaper (glasspaper) and rub them together.

Hoofbeats Take two halves of a coconut shell and either strike them together or drum them upon a plaster wall. If you cover them with cloth you can imitate hoofbeats on a soft surface.

Footfalls In the forest: rhythmically crush a handful of old recording tape in front of the microphone.
In the snow: do the same with a small bag of flour.

Bird's wings Small bird: let a small piece of card flutter against an electric fan.
Large bird: rhythmically swish two pieces of bamboo cane in front of the microphone.

Jet plane Run a hairdryer or vacuum cleaner near the microphone and make it howl by restricting the exhaust.

Gun shot Strike a table or a leather chair seat with a ruler or cane.

A telephone voice Method one: speak into a small plastic or earthenware cup.
Method two: plug some headphones into the microphone input and speak into them. If the impedances are reasonably correct the headphone diaphragm corresponds in performance to the cheap microphone in a telephone.

ORDERING EFFECTS FROM A SOUND LIBRARY

In order to save yourself time, money and general heartache a comprehensive and detailed list should be compiled before you approach a library. The director will say what effects he requires but it is up to the sound man to interpret these in practical terms. First you must plan how many cues on how many tapes you will require.

If the sound track is at all complicated then at least two playback units will be required. Place all the important spot cues on one tape (assuming that there is no danger of overlapping) and all the general backgrounds on another. This is not only more logical in operation but in the event of a deck failure all the vital cues are still available.

Any cues of indeterminate length where there is danger of running into the next effect should be kept on the second or third tape. Always

allow extra running time if in doubt as it is a simple matter to prune the tape in rehearsals.

First make a list of cues in the order required on the reels required with their timings. The library technician, who knows nothing about your particular production, will also need a detailed description of each effect. It is no good specifying 'church clock strikes four': is it small, large, town, country, with Westminster chimes, with simpler chimes, without chimes, near, distant, fast, slow, high, low?

You may also wish to specify a different coloured leader tape between certain cues for ease of location in rehearsals. And you must certainly specify the tape speed and the track configuration.

It was difficult to know what to do with some requests we have received for sound effects. For instance, one stage manager wrote ordering 'five minutes of almost recorded silence — like you get in the country'. A dear lady replying to our request for more specific details such as the duration of her cues and the required tape speed ended her letter with '. . . and as for the speed of tape, I think fairly slow'. One customer took our plea for 'as much information as possible' to heart. We have on file his letter requesting five cues of pigs grunting and/or squealing: it goes on for four closely typed pages. We not only had a good idea what the entire play was about, but knew how many pigs were in the sty, what their age range was, their sex, how they felt about the possibility of food, how they felt about the possibility — then probability — of death by the knife, how some panicked when the assassin entered and some remained calm, and so on and so forth. I am also very fond of the letter from a vicar staging an amateur production in the church hall; he wanted 'the sound effect of a cock crowing (*thrice*)'.

MONO, TWIN-TRACK OR STEREO

Because one is usually putting a single sound on to a single loudspeaker theatre recordings are more often than not monaural. But there are exceptions. Theoretically with loudspeakers placed widely apart at both sides of a proscenium arch stereo music recordings should not work. The loudspeakers are supposed to be within an angle of not more than 30 degrees and equidistant from the listener. However, I

"TITLE OF PRODUCTION"   -   MUSIC AND EFFECTS

CUE	TIMING	TAPE A	TAPE B	TAPE C	DESCRIPTION
1.	30"	Curtain Music			Disc: LP 3012 Side 1 Band 2 from start of theme after 20sec. intro.
2.	3' 00"		Crowd -(Happy)		Approx. 500 talking, shouting in town square.
3.	12"	Crowd Cheer 1			Big cheer fr popular leader (Same crowd as 2)
4.	5"	Crowd Cheer 2			Bigger cheer
5.	4' 00"			Crowd (Angry)	Same crowd – verging on riot.
6.	5"	Crowd Shout 1			Angry shouts of protest.
7.	10"	Crowd Shout 2			Same with booing and jeering added.
8.	15"		Police Sirens		2 or 3 modern British police cars arrive. (No brakes a sirens)
9.	8"	Gun Shots			Machine gun (2sec) then 5/6 sporadic pistol shots.
10.	5"	Explosion			Car petrol tank blows up.
11.	6"	Ambulance			Ambulance arrives with siren and squealing tyres.
12.	2' 00"	Scene Music			Disc: LP 3012 Side 2 Band 1 from start.
13.	6' 00"		Birds		2 or 3. English countryside. Hot summer afternoon.
14.	15"	Dog			Farm dog (Collie?) barks at stranger.

Fig 70 Typical working list of music and effects

80

have found that in most cases music is definitely enhanced by being recorded in stereo.

Stereo can also be useful for providing breadth and perspective to crowd, battle, traffic, sea effects, etc. Moving sounds like cars, aeroplanes and trains can, of course, be recorded in stereo, but will be fixed in their timing. It is much more flexible to have the same mono sound on twin tracks fed separately to two loudspeakers. Then, by adjusting the relative gains, the effect can be moved from one loudspeaker to the other at will.

Twin tracks may also be used for two different continuous effects of indeterminate length; for example, rain on one track and wind on the other. This would leave a second tape machine free for spot effects.

Mock stereo effects can be made up on twin-tracks for synchronous playback. For example I once created a good 'theatrical' sea effect by recording waves crashing on to the beach on the upper track and deep sucking undertow noises on the lower track. In the theatre the crashing of waves from loudspeakers on stage was followed by a quieter undertow sound within the auditorium. This gave the effect of water advancing and retreating. Incidentally, the wave was made up from a constant heavy waterfall with sharp increases of level and treble for each crash; and the undertow noise was several loops of various water effects at half and quarter speed. Real sea recordings did not sound half as convincing.

A similar technique was used in *Othello* at the Old Vic in London, 1963, when the director requested a rapid tolling bell which was somehow to build into an insistent mind-tormenting noise. So on one track there was an ordinary bell which began the sequence and on the other was a short loop of some of the reverberation of the same bell played backwards. This loop produced an unpleasant rising stabbing sound. It was gradually faded up during a period of intensive action on the stage until, at its height, it had taken over from the original bell. Thus the bell was 'transformed' into a surrealistic effect.

A very convincing thunder effect was achieved for another production by recording thunder crashing on one track and rumbling on the other. In the theatre the initial crash was played on large loudspeakers high up in the auditorium followed by the rumble fading away on loudspeakers on stage. The feeling of perspective and distance was remarkable.

EXAMPLES OF THE CREATION OF RECORDED EFFECTS

At this point it is worth looking at a few more practical examples of the creation of sound effects, the problems encountered and the techniques used to solve them.

THE BATTLE OF TRAFALGAR

At Madame Tussaud's Waxworks Exhibition in London there is a life-sized and faithful reconstruction of part of the lower gun deck of HMS *Victory* at the height of the battle of Trafalgar. In the Orlop deck below is the famous tableau of the death of Lord Nelson. On the gun deck there are lighting effects, flashes, smoke and even the smell of tar and cordite. The six synchronized sound tracks include the roar of cannons, the shouts and cries of men, a falling mast, cannonballs crashing through timber, musket fire, naval commands, return fire from the enemy, bugles blowing 'cease fire', etc. (photographs 33 and 34).

When we were asked to create the sound of Trafalgar (in 1968) we were lucky enough to have the cooperation of the then captain of the *Victory*, the ship being in permanent dry-dock at Portsmouth. About a dozen naval ratings were pressed into becoming our guncrew for the afternoon and, complete with shouted commands from an authentic gun-drill of the period, we were able to record the massive lumbering cannon being loaded, run out and aimed.

Later the Royal Navy Gunnery School, who after a slow start because of red tape and insurance problems became more than enthusiastic, actually fired several rounds using one of *Victory*'s guns which stands on the quay beside the ship. The correct loading, aiming and firing drill was carried out; there was a drummer 'beating to quarters' and the navy had even gone to the trouble of providing papier mâché cannonballs.

As this was possibly the last time that one of these guns would ever be fired we made sure that we were well covered for equipment. The plan was to use different types of microphones at varying distances from the gun to obtain a selection of perspectives.

My colleague, Tony Horder, and myself positioned ourselves very efficiently with our headsets on and our best microphones and equipment carefully placed and ready. But there was one very old EMI-L2 tape machine left over with an equally old and battered Grampian moving coil microphone. So I set the record control at almost nil and asked a willing helper to take it a little way off, point the microphone in the general direction of the cannon and switch the machine on before the bang. Needless to say this was the most effective recording we obtained. It was used in the final programme as the main explosions of nearby guns, while the other recordings provided a whole spectrum of cannon fire for the general background.

The day preceding the session on board *Victory* we actually went to sea in a yacht to record sounds of timber creaking, rope through tackle, canvas flapping and water running against timber. We also went on board *Foudroyant* which is the oldest wooden warship still afloat.

All this is the fun part of location recording. But because of the various hazards previously discussed we ended up with many reels of tape of interesting atmospheric sounds, but very few clean effects. And it was at this point that the work really began. After days of sifting through the tapes the basic sounds finally came from the following sources:

Gunfire Location HMS *Victory*

Gun being run out. Location HMS *Victory*

Gun orders Studio with hoarse friends (aided by a little alcohol).

Shouts, cries, screams Studio with hoarser friends (aided by a lot of alcohol, and later drastically edited).

Other orders Studio

Bosun's call (*whistle*) Studio

Ropes, tackle, etc. Fly gallery in an empty theatre

Musket fire Library muskets plus a crackerjack firework, which sounds remarkably similar.

Sea sounds Library

Timber creaking Squeaky chair at quarter speed

Ropes creaking Squeaky door at half speed

Thumps and crashes Wooden boxes, heavy weights, chairs and tables hurled around the studio. The result carefully edited and played

at various speeds either forwards or backwards depending upon which sounded more interesting.

Mast falling A bit of creaking from a library effect of tree-felling, into more creaking from breaking a piece of wood in the studio (half speed), into a selection of carefully edited thumps and crashes from previous session.

Enemy ship alongside A really deep thump for the initial impact followed by a scraping sound made by a large wooden sliding door. The door was slightly warped and made a marvellous noise, especially when played back at half speed.

Enemy cannonball A sharp crack and splinter of wood recorded in the studio, edited on to a rasping-scrape made by dragging a wooden crate filled with heavy weights along a concrete floor, edited on to general crashes and thumps. The finished effect, lasting only about three seconds, gives the impression of a heavy lump of metal bursting through the wooden side of a ship and crashing along the deck. A few shouts and screams complete the picture.

Fire crackle Library

Running feet Bare feet running on the wooden deck of a ship were actually recorded on board *Foudroyant*. This was meant to be the fire party rushing to deal with a small fire. Unfortunately bare feet did not sound very dramatic and a library effect (with boots) was used.

Nearest gun When a large gun is fired the force of the explosion makes it leap backwards. Naval guns of the period were fitted with heavy chains to restrain this vicious recoil. To recreate as authentic a sound as possible we recorded some chain being whipped tight, and edited on to this a particularly hefty thud recorded on *Victory* when they were heaving one of the cannons into position. These two effects were mixed with the best cannon sound. The resulting sequence is of an almighty explosion with the clink of the restraining chains as the gun leaps backwards followed by a heavy thud as it comes crashing down on to the deck.

So although tremendous time and effort went into trying to record the real sounds, they were mostly used for reference. A good 75 per cent of the finished sound track had to be fabricated.

HENRY V

Another interesting example of making up a complicated composite effect was for John Barton's production of *Henry V* for the Royal Shakespeare Company at Stratford Upon Avon in 1966. In that season the repertoire included all of Shakespeare's historical plays in sequence. These included so many fights and battle scenes that by the time we reached the first battle in *Henry V* every trick in the book had been pulled. It was therefore decided that the battle of Harfleur should be recreated in sound alone with a darkened stage and no actors or scenery. In fact the idea does spring directly from the text. At the beginning of the play the Chorus addresses the following lines to audience :

Piece out our imperfections with your thoughts :
Into a thousand parts divide one man.
And make imaginary puissance ;
Think, when we talk of horses that you see them
Printing their proud hoofs i' th' receiving earth ;
For 'tis your thoughts that now must deck
our kings. . . .

Given this lead we went to work to produce a battle in the mind. First to collect the ingredients. Guy Woolfenden, musical director of the R.S.C., had created what he called his 'sword noise'. This had backed up all previous fight sequences in the season and so it was decided to incorporate it in order to maintain style. The sword noise was a particularly unpleasant and penetrating metallic sound made by bowing with violin bows on cymbals. I had some good arrow swishes recorded with a bamboo cane and repeated in a tightly edited sequence to sound like a flight. We also had a copy of what has become accepted as standard arrow noise from Laurence Olivier's wartime film of *Henry V*. Incidentally, he once told me that this 'authentic' flight of arrows was actually made by looping an elastic band round the needle of one of the studio's big old fashioned gramophones and twanging it. (Not to be recommended on our modern and more delicate equipment!) The sound which came out of the loudspeaker was a marvellous twangy-swishing effect of hundreds of archers firing in volleys.

Other ingredients immediately available were some very good screams and shouts recorded with the actors, stock crowd effects, sword clashing recorded with the actual prop swords, horses neighing, thundering hoofbeats and various French and English trumpet calls and flourishes specially composed and recorded by Guy Woolfenden.

It was decided to make the start of the battle as realistic as possible and then, as the director put it, to 'go nasty'. The end of the sequence would meld back to normality with the lights and the actors and the resumption of the play.

Two things were missing : a tension-getting sound preceding the battle to be building during the Chorus speech, and some unreal and nasty arrow noises. The first was manufactured by recording a continuous bowing on a tam-tam (large oriental gong) which, rather like running a wet finger round the rim of a glass, builds and builds the more you bow. Played back at a quarter speed the effect was of a deep singing roar growing relentlessly in pitch and intensity.

The 'nasty arrows' were eventually created at about 4.30 in the morning by viciously scraping piano strings with a coin. The resulting metallic screeches rising in tone were played backwards to obtain descending notes, and were then tightly chopped together to match up with the bamboo cane flights of arrows.

Our four minute battle when complete used four tape machines ; one for the tam-tam effect and three for the specific sounds. These three tapes were carefully timed with prerecorded fades and blank coloured leaders inserted when pauses or speaker switching were called for. Even so, the sound operator had to memorize the many volume settings and loudspeaker changes throughout the sequence.

The pattern of events was broadly, as follows : tam-tam building imperceptibly under Chorus speech ; then during last line of speech ('. . . eke out our performance with your mind') thundering hoofbeats can be heard approaching from upstage centre ; at the end of the speech the lights fade out on the lone figure centre stage, and the hoofbeats build to a crescendo ; suddenly there is a flight of arrows loud from the rear of the auditorium and the scream of a horse in agony on stage ; then immediately, filling the entire theatre, the ferocious impact of two armies meeting head on with the clash of arms, fearsome shouts, horses, bugles, arrows, and all hell let loose ; the real arrows gradually turn into metallic arrows and the screeching sword noise takes over from the battle effects ; the tam-tam, running throughout, has by now built up

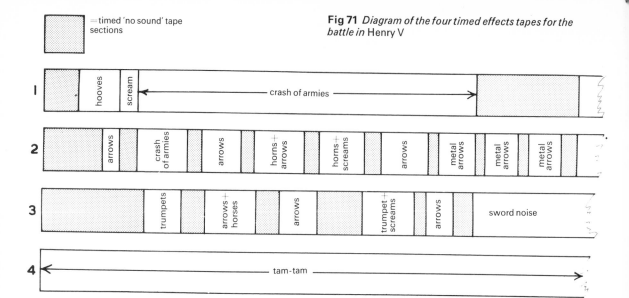

=timed 'no sound' tape sections

Fig 71 *Diagram of the four timed effects tapes for the battle in* Henry V

1 | hooves | scream | ← crash of armies → |

2 | arrows | crash of armies | arrows | horns + arrows | horns + screams | arrows | metal arrows | metal arrows | metal arrows |

3 | trumpets | arrows + horses | arrows | trumpet + screams | arrows | sword noise |

4 ← tam-tam →

to a high-pitched whine; when everybody in the audience has their teeth well and truly set on edge the metallic horror sound in the auditorium fades down leaving a realistic battle noise on stage. Thus the focus is brought back to the action.

BLITZ

In 1962 at the Adelphi theatre in London there was a musical which was a sound man's dream. Written by Lionel Bart (of *Oliver* fame) it was set in wartime London during the worst period of bombing. Aptly enough, the show was called *Blitz*.

As far as I can ascertain it was the first West End production to have a specially designed and built sound effects mixing console. This was fairly basic by today's standards but seemed very daring at the time. It consisted of three sets of remote starts and gain controls for the tape machines, switching of any combination of tape machines to any combination of four main 'group' faders (each controlling a 100 watt amplifier), and fourteen loudspeaker circuits with individual on/off switches and selection to any one of the amplifiers.

The research for the show was extremely interesting as much of the sound track had to be genuine archive material. We used BBC recordings of wartime news bulletins and radio pro-

grammes, Lord Haw-Haw broadcasting propaganda from Germany and some extracts from Churchill's famous speeches. From Pathé news and other film libraries we obtained genuine wartime recordings of the Blitz itself.

But, as is usual, most of the finished tracks had to be fabricated in the interests of a good 'clean' tape. For example, the film recording of a German bomber was very good and very exciting, but unusable because of the background and surface noise. A substitute was created by taking a more modern aeroplane recording and slowing it down until it matched the sinister pitch.

The climax of the first act was a full-scale raid on London. This started with a distant air raid siren echoed by one closer, then another and then one in the auditorium. Next came distant anti-aircraft gunfire followed by nearer gunfire and the drone of enemy aircraft. From that point on it built up into a cacophony of bombs, guns, aircraft, buildings falling down, fire engines and ambulance bells. At its peak the four 100 watt amplifiers managed to top a thirty piece orchestra playing flat out.

The lighting effects, with flame projectors, searchlights, smoke bombs and flashes, were handled by Richard Pilbrow and we carefully worked out our sequence of flashes and bangs so that they would not only coincide but come from the right area of the stage.

I used a similar technique to that used later in

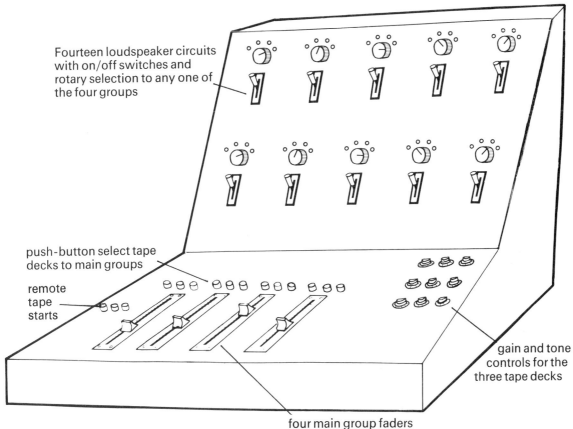

Fourteen loudspeaker circuits with on/off switches and rotary selection to any one of the four groups

push-button select tape decks to main groups

remote tape starts

gain and tone controls for the three tape decks

four main group faders

Fig 72 *Sound effects mixer built for* Blitz (*1962*)

Henry V in that one tape consisted of air raid siren into general blitz and the other two were air raid sirens into an assortment of spot effects. The general background was played through three large loudspeakers incorporating 18 in. (457 mm) bass units on stage, and the others were switched frantically around so that an aeroplane would appear audience left, a bomb would drop up stage right, an ambulance down stage left, a bomb up centre, ack ack down stage right, a building collapse up stage left, and so on. Throughout all this the orchestra was playing, the stage setting was constantly changing, and the actors were rushing about in general confusion putting out fires, taking cover and rescuing people with ladders from second storey windows.

There was one other interesting innovation in that show. The basic stage setting consisted of two 30 foot (about 9 m) steel towers spanned by a steel bridge nearly the width of the proscenium arch. Not only could this bridge go from stage floor level to thirty feet up, but the entire four ton motorized unit could track from the back of the stage to the front. As if this were not enough of a stage manager's nightmare, there were also four two ton steel structures representing three storey buildings which were capable of moving freely about the stage. Each one measured approximately 24 feet (7·5 m) high with a base 5 × 10 feet (about 1·5 × 3 m). The units were battery powered with the controls set in a small camouflaged cabin in the centre. The stage managers responsible for these juggernauts could, with the aid of a few push buttons and a steering wheel, drive them forwards or backwards. And they could also revolve the entire structure about them.

Take all these free ranging pieces and add a great deal of fixed-position flying scenery and lighting, plus a cast of nearly forty people, and it is obvious that the strictest technical control is necessary. Again as far as I have been able to discover, this was the first West End show to use a radio system for the technicians. The complexities of the production called for two technical stage managers working in unison. It worked out as follows: stage manager A was positioned on the non-working-side fly gallery with a microphone and radio transmitter (photograph 35). From this vantage-point he could operate the massive bridge, making sure that the other mobile units were not in the way. He gave verbal cues and general instructions to the four drivers via individual radio receivers, and similarly cued all the flying. Stage manager B was in the traditional prompt corner position with the prompt script, giving all the lighting, follow spots and special effects cues via cue-lights and a normal loudspeaker paging system. He was also equipped with a radio receiver in order to be able to synchronize with stage manager A, while he in his turn could hear stage manager B via a paging loudspeaker on the fly gallery.

All in all, it was a show which relied somewhat heavily upon sound (and I have not even mentioned the reinforcement system).

LOUDSPEAKER PLACEMENT

When placing effects loudspeakers on a stage one must ensure that they are in the correct location for the illusion required, that they are facing the audience and that they are not behind anything which is not acoustically transparent.

Illusion of sound source In a large auditorium of a conventional proscenium theatre only the first few rows will be conscious of whether the sound is coming from upstage left or upstage right. However, because the angles become more obtuse, downstage positions are more critical. The 15 degree horizontal angle of directivity of the human ear is a good rule of thumb to follow. Since the ear is not so discriminating in a vertical plane it might be more convenient to mount the speakers above stage level.

If a sound is meant to be coming from a prop radio, television, etc., on stage, every effort should be made to place a small loudspeaker either in the prop or built in to the scenery nearby. If this is not practical then the loudspeaker used should be in a line with the audience, behind and slightly to one side of the prop.

Facing the audience It has been previously stressed that the higher frequencies provide crispness and clarity. And as high frequencies are directional and do not travel round corners it is essential to mount loudspeakers so that they are facing the audience. Again because high frequencies are directional this will assist the audience to locate the source of sound. If a loudspeaker is on one side of a stage but pointing at only one section of the audience that section will hear a clear sound from an obvious source. The rest of the audience will hear, in varying degrees, a blurred sound from no distinct source.

Problems of masking In almost every instance loudspeakers on a stage have to be masked from the audience, and this is where compromises may have to be made. With a little forethought and some cooperation from the set designer, however, it is usually possible to find a satisfactory solution.

A definition of 'acoustically transparent' is a perforated material which is at least 50 per cent open. Gauze (or scrim) is all right, and some open weave hessians (burlap) of the non-hairy variety are passable. All brands of loudspeaker material are, of course, ideal. Scenic canvas is not acceptable, and painted scenic canvas is even less so. Drapes or heavy curtain materials are to be avoided at all costs.

When arranging for a hole to be made in the scenery for the loudspeaker remember that it need not be the size of the entire cabinet. Ideally, all of the cone (or cones) should be free. However, as long as the high frequency section is completely open it might be acceptable to mask, say, a third of the bass unit.

I once did a play with a particular musical effect which sounded perfectly all right when played during a sound rehearsal, but always sounded dull and muffled during the dress rehearsals. The reason for this puzzling phenomenon was eventually discovered. An elderly actor wearing a heavy and voluminous robe was using the loudspeaker as a resting place between entrances. On another occasion I had similar trouble from a party of 'nuns'. But this time I was forewarned and took immediate steps. The loudspeaker was suspended off the ground to above head height.

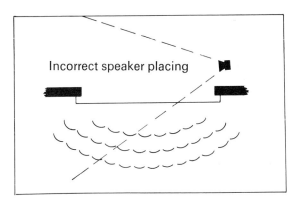

Incorrect speaker placing

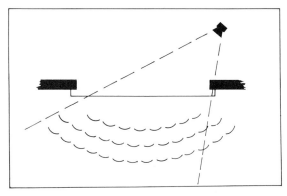

Fig 73 *Effects loudspeakers should face the audience*

SETTING LEVELS

If the control position is properly placed within the auditorium then the setting of sound levels is purely a matter of discussion between the operator and the director. The sound man will note the director's wishes and balance the sound with the action accordingly.

If the control position is backstage or in an enclosed box then the matter becomes more complicated. In this case it is important that the sound operator is able to equate what he is hearing with what is going on in the auditorium. He should therefore, as a first step, set up a selection of quiet cues so that they are only just discernible in the auditorium. He should then go back to the operating position to judge the difference.

When working from backstage one is likely to be near a loudspeaker and it will probably be found that an effect which seems quite loud is hardly audible out front. So when plotting levels note the actual setting where the sound first becomes audible to the audience. Thus the cue might read fade from $2\frac{1}{2}$–5′ rather than '0–5′, in which case the cue will appear on time rather than a fraction late.

Level setting should always be carried out with the correct stage settings in case there are problems of masking loudspeakers or of very absorbent or reflective surfaces.

It is also pointless trying to judge a balance unless the theatre is quiet. Arrange a time when all the noisy people (carpenters and lighting men) have gone to lunch.

Finally, it is worth remembering that when the auditorium is full of people you can probably afford to bring all the sound levels up a touch, since bodies in clothes tend to absorb sound.

PLOTS OR CUE-SHEETS

There are no rules about how one should make out a plot or cue-sheet but there are rules regarding the content. A good plot should:
1 Be clear and logical to follow.
2 Tell you what to do next (whether it be a preset or a cue).
3 Indicate the state of the equipment at any given point.
4 Be as precise and concise as possible.
And it should be all these things before the final dress rehearsals.

Some people prefer to put everything down in columns; for example, Cue – Effect – Tape – Gain – Loudspeaker – Notes. The 'notes' column is used for alterations in tone setting, any specific remarks about changes in volume levels, tricky speaker switching, etc.

I usually like to use a different colour ink for each tape deck and a third very definite colour for all presetting of controls. Presets should be plotted as carefully as the actual cues. In the excitement of a first night it is sometimes difficult to work out whether or not it is safe to, say, switch a speaker on or off on one output channel while an effect is still running on another.

An alternative method is to make a basic cue-sheet consisting of a simple diagram of the control layout leaving space for the cueline and notes. This system requires a separate sheet for every cue but it has the advantage of speed in plotting. It is also very easy to change. Each sheet is a complete record of the state of all the controls at that point. The disadvantage is when one comes to a long sequence of complicated manoeuvres.

Personally I prefer a variation of the first method. I prepare neatly photocopied blank sheets ruled out in columns and insert them between each page of a script in a ring binder. I like to have a script because a sound operator should take his own cues except when technical problems of synchronization make a cue from the stage manager necessary. It is not possible to place a sound into the action of a play with any kind of feeling if you are doing it second hand.

The columns in my cue-sheets vary with the equipment in use and the complexity of the show. If, for example, three tape decks are concurrently in use a great deal of the time I will certainly plot their starts, stops and level changes in separate columns. This will provide an immediate visual indication of what should be happening with each deck. Alternatively, if the production calls for complicated manoeuvring and routing of mainly one tape machine

with a second being used only occasionally for general background effects, then the cuesheet would be tailored accordingly. In this instance the group output faders and the loudspeaker switching would feature heavily in the columns.

On a long running show the plot will become unnecessary after a number of performances but I would strongly advocate preparing a shorthand version on a single sheet to be always at hand. Just as an actor can fluff a line on the hundredth performance a technician can suffer a similar blank.

I also use a number of abbreviations and signs when plotting to keep the instructions concise. Some of these are standard music notation and some have been evolved from my own experience.

⌒	music notation for a pause
<8	music notation for growing louder
>2	music notation for growing softer
	(The number is added to denote a gain setting control.)
SNAP 6	bring gain smartly to that level

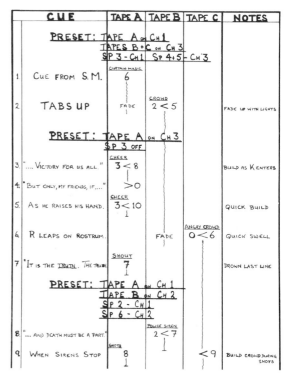

Fig 74 *Cue sheets. Two methods of plotting the same sequence.*

0–6	start at 0 and bring smoothly to 6
3–6	start at 3 and bring smoothly to 6
Slow 3–6	start at 3 and fade slowly to 6
Fade	fade effect smoothly out
Slow fade	fade effect slowly out
CUT	Cut the effect
Sp	Loudspeaker
Mc	Microphone
T/T	Disc turntable
Ch	Channel

LIVE AND MECHANICAL EFFECTS

Certain sounds will always be more convincingly produced 'live' or manually. For various reasons either the microphone is unable to capture the essence of the sound, or the loudspeaker is incapable of reproducing it. For example, a pistol shot is always much more effective with a blank cartridge in a real gun. Even a good thwack on a leather chair seat with a cane can have more immediacy than a recorded gun shot. And door bells, phone bells, door chimes and door knockers are usually more easily done live. Glass and crockery crashes are also better with the real thing.

To achieve a really loud explosion which will make the audience jump out of their seats there is no substitute for a 'bomb'. This is literally a large firework, obtainable from lighting equipment hire companies, which is set off by connecting it to a mains supply and throwing the switch. The bomb must always be suspended in a large galvanized tank with a wire mesh cover. This 'bomb tank' should be placed understage or somewhere where the actors and technicians are not liable to be at the moment of detonation. Since it is a very short sharp explosion it is often desirable to back it up with a taped effect for added realism.

The best rain effect I have ever heard in the theatre was actually rigged for visual reasons. A perforated water pipe was suspended horizontally about 10 feet (3 m) high behind a window in the set. Below the window, masked from the audience, was a long canvas trough with a runaway at one end. The idea was to side-light the falling drops of water and let the audience actually see the rain. The bonus for us was that the sound the water made hitting the canvas was superb. Later we tried to record it, but it sounded totally unconvincing when reproduced electronically.

An effect I would very much like to experience is of one of the old thunder runs. Theatres such as the Bristol Old Vic still have these long gently sloping wooden chutes running down from the flies. The effect, which apparently rumbled and shook the entire building, was achieved by letting large solid iron cannonballs roll down the chute. Extra vibrations were created by ridges at irregular intervals which made the cannonballs jump.

The Moscow Arts Theatre on a visit to London some years ago achieved a similar effect by rolling heavy weights around in the wings. They also brought with them two very realistic rain machines, one for light rain and one for a downpour. The first was a wire-sided wooden drum on edge with revolving paddles inside which scooped up and let drop fragments of cartridge paper. The stagehand turning the paddles could produce either a continuous or undulating swishing sound. The other machine was a smaller revolving drum with three sets of spaced ridges. As the drum revolved each ridge in turn came into contact with three fixed strips of heavy leather. Each strip of leather was lifted and then allowed to 'thwack' back. This produced an effect of heavy drops of rain falling at whatever speed the drum was revolved. The two machines together in a carefully rehearsed sequence were spectacular.

One of the most famous of all sound effects was for *The Ghost Train* by Arnold Ridley. First produced at the St Martins Theatre in London in 1925, it is still a firm favourite with repertory and amateur companies. I can do no better than quote the actual stage directions as they appear in French's acting edition of the script:

THE GHOST TRAIN

1 tubular bell (E flat).
1 garden roller propelled over bevel-edged struts screwed to stage, 30 inches apart.
1 18-gallon galvanized iron tank.
1 thunder-sheet.
Air cylinders (obtainable from British Oxygen Co., Wembley, or local agents).
1 bass *rope* drum and pair of sticks.

2 side-drums.
1 small padded mallet (auctioneer's hammer).
1 large padded mallet (for beating tank).
1 medium mallet.
1 wire-drum brush.
1 milk-churn.
1 pea-whistle.
1 train whistle (for mouth).
1 whistle on cylinder.
2 electric or hand-driven motors.
2 slides cut to give shadows of carriage windows of train.
2 flood arcs on each side *of stage*.
1 tin amplifier for steam with a counterweight placed in its mouth.

TO WORK FIRST TRAIN

Screw whistle into nozzle of cylinder.
1 man sits astride this and another cylinder with amplifier ready to work (A).
1 man stands by roller (B).
1 man stands by tank with large padded mallet (C).
1 man stands by thunder-sheet (D).
2 men stand by motors (E).
2 men stand by flood arcs with slides focused on exterior of windows (F).
1 man stands by with wire brush and small side drum (G).
1 man stands by bass drum (H).

On the rise of the curtain the Stage Manager hits the tubular bell twice with small padded mallet. When Stationmaster lights gas, C and H beat on tank and drum gently, gradually increasing in volume. Then E and G start, followed by D. Finally A starts air release, and as the total volume of sounds increases, B starts to pull his roller over the struts as rapidly as possible, gradually slowing. When noise is at its height, all *stop dead* except A, who continues to blow off air. While train is in station, Stationmaster shouts 'All change!' 'All change!' while C repeatedly beats milk-churn with its lid. He stops as Stage Manager blows pea-whistle. A gives two sharp blasts on his whistle (H has carried his bass drum to O.P. (R) side of stage while train is in station). Stage Manager then grasps medium padded mallet and beats second side-drum (which should be fairly slack) 1 beat. Then another beat, then another, gradually increasing in pace and diminishing in

volume as train is supposed to leave station. *Simultaneously, and keeping in time with him*, D gives a shake to sheet, A gives puff of steam, B gives beat on tank, E works motors and B starts roller. H also does roll on drum. These effects should be carried on until noise of train dies away in the distance in an indistinct murmur. As train leaves station F slide their slides across the window in turn, gradually increasing in pace to give the effect of the train lights passing the waiting-rooms. *The whole success of the Effect depends on each unit being together and the rhythm preserved*.

TO WORK SECOND TRAIN

In this train it is necessary to have three cue lights fixed so that all the effects men can see them. The switches should be in prompt corner. When the Stage Manager blows whistle for train in distance C and H start as in the first train, E then starts with G, then D joins in. When Peggy says 'It's coming! It's coming!' and runs to Charles, Stage Manager should switch on his first cue light. This should bring A with steam, and other effects, except B, to nearly forte. When Julia turns to run up to window, he switches on second cue light. This should bring in *all* effects double forte, including B and A's whistle. When Julia throws bottle through window, an amber flare followed by flash-box, on P.S. (L) window, fractional pause, then amber flare and flash-box through O.P. (R) window. When Julia falls, bring curtain down. At end of first picture switch on third cue light. On this, all effects must *stop dead*.

TO WORK THIRD TRAIN

Only A, B, E, G and H are required for this train. B works his roller over the bare stage in this effect and *NOT* over the struts.
When Teddie shoots at Price in doorway, the Stage Manager blows his train-whistle (mouth), H starts gently on drum, giving beat of a train puffing up hill. A and G keep time with him. The sound gradually increases until Teddie exits. When it comes up to forte but still maintains its steady beat B joins in. When Teddie re-enters, the train rapidly dies away to silence.

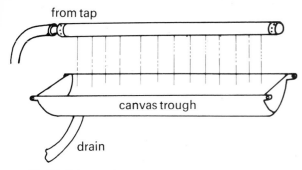

from tap

canvas trough

drain

Fig 75 *Rain trough*

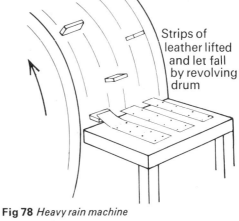

Strips of leather lifted and let fall by revolving drum

Fig 78 *Heavy rain machine*

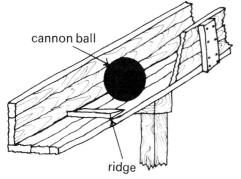

cannon ball

ridge

Fig 76 *Thunder run*

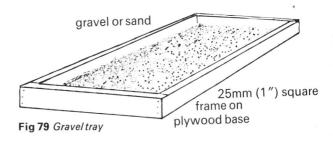

gravel or sand

25mm (1″) square frame on plywood base

Fig 79 *Gravel tray*

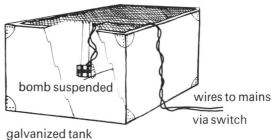

wire mesh securely fixed

bomb suspended

wires to mains via switch

galvanized tank

Fig 80 *Bomb tank*

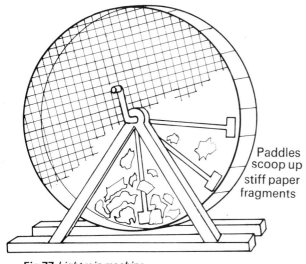

Paddles scoop up stiff paper fragments

Fig 77 *Light rain machine*

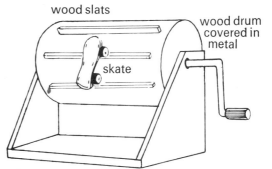

wood slats

wood drum covered in metal

skate

Use side of drum off slats for a cart on a hard surface

Fig 81 *Train machine*

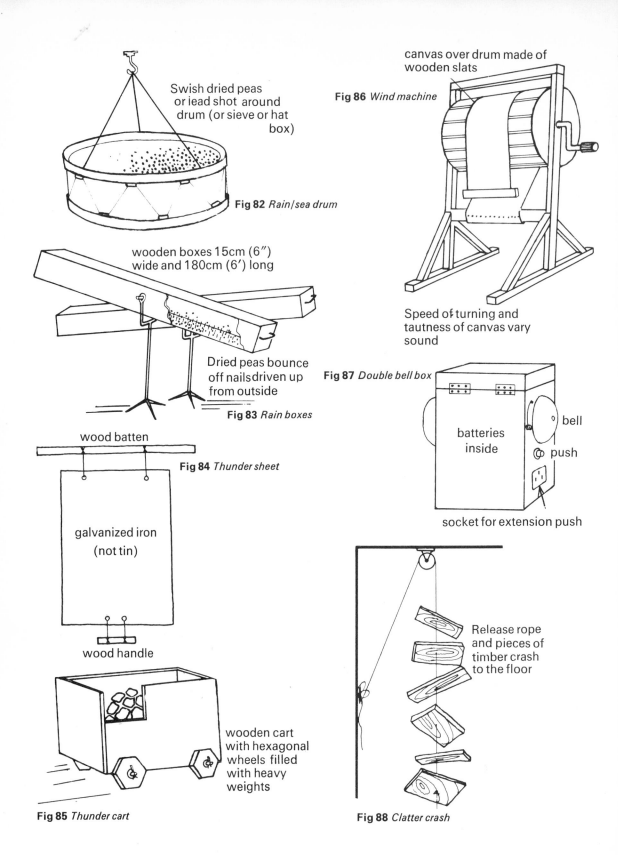

Swish dried peas or iead shot around drum (or sieve or hat box)

Fig 82 *Rain/sea drum*

wooden boxes 15cm (6″) wide and 180cm (6′) long

Dried peas bounce off nails driven up from outside

Fig 83 *Rain boxes*

wood batten

Fig 84 *Thunder sheet*

galvanized iron (not tin)

wood handle

wooden cart with hexagonal wheels filled with heavy weights

Fig 85 *Thunder cart*

canvas over drum made of wooden slats

Fig 86 *Wind machine*

Speed of turning and tautness of canvas vary sound

Fig 87 *Double bell box*

batteries inside

bell

push

socket for extension push

Release rope and pieces of timber crash to the floor

Fig 88 *Clatter crash*

Fig 89 *Whip*

Smack plywood whip against firm object

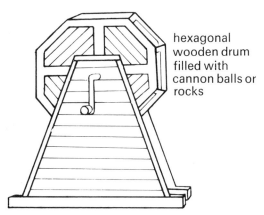

Fig 90 *Avalanche machine*

hexagonal wooden drum filled with cannon balls or rocks

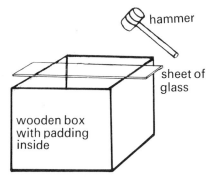

hammer

sheet of glass

wooden box with padding inside

Fig 91 *Glass crash*

wire netting covered with cloth

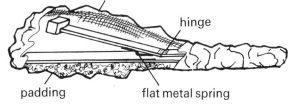

hinge

padding

flat metal spring

Strike on padded plywood base away from wooden knocker which will hit plywood and spring away

Fig 92 *Comedy club*

Fig 93 *Cork popper*

bicycle pump with end removed to fit cork

Hold stiff paper in blades of electric fan

Fig 94 *Bird wings*

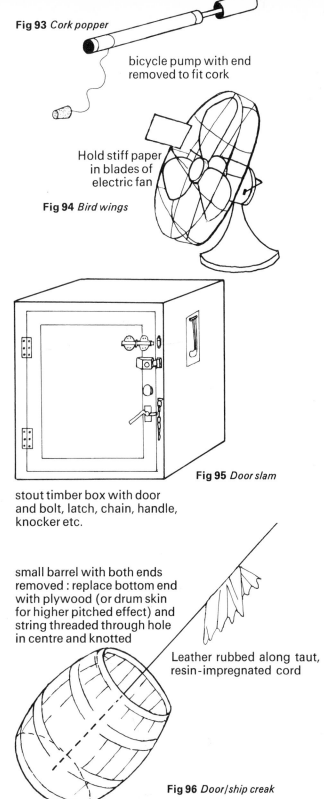

Fig 95 *Door slam*

stout timber box with door and bolt, latch, chain, handle, knocker etc.

small barrel with both ends removed : replace bottom end with plywood (or drum skin for higher pitched effect) and string threaded through hole in centre and knotted

Leather rubbed along taut, resin-impregnated cord

Fig 96 *Door/ship creak*

12 Sound reinforcement

ACOUSTICS

Before discussing electronic sound reinforcement a few basic facts about acoustics will be helpful. The rules of acoustics are simple but the situations and factors affecting them are endless.

The object of theatre acoustics is to project the sound of the performance on stage out to the entire audience, and to have it arrive everywhere at the same time and with the same characteristics of spectrum and intensity.

This ideal state of affairs is for many reasons extremely difficult to achieve. For instance, except in the case of a solo performer, the sound source can be anywhere in the stage area. We may also be dealing with a number of sources at the same time. Furthermore the sound from these sources will arrive at the listener's ear having travelled many different paths.

Apart from a certain amount of direct sound most will reach the listener by reflecting off ceilings and walls (sometimes even floors); in fact, off all surfaces to a greater or lesser extent. In a badly designed auditorium sound may reach the listener after having been reflected back and forth across the auditorium several times. This is why most good auditoria combine various features for combating multiple echoes, such as non-symmetrical walls, soft absorbent rear walls, curved boxes, convex balcony fascia and ceilings sloping down towards the back of the house.

Reflections within the stage area must also be taken into account. The hard brick walls of an empty stage will set up undesirable multiple reflections, and the relatively small area of the proscenium opening will allow only a minor percentage of the energy through. A box set, on the other hand, will help to project the sound into the auditorium. If the fly tower above the box set is full of scenery and drapes this will absorb a great deal of the energy but it will also help to eliminate unwanted reverberations. So

the pros will outweigh the cons.

Sound will continue to be reflected around in an enclosed environment until it is absorbed. Smooth hard surfaces like plaster, brick, concrete, plywood and metal will reflect efficiently and absorb little. Scenic materials will reflect in proportion to their stiffness and hardness; a painted canvas backdrop, for example, will assist the projection of sound, while a heavy velour backdrop will not.

Most theatres built for plays and musicals are moderately live, i.e. they have a large area of hard interior surface, and they are often excessively reverberant when the house is empty. Cinemas are acoustically designed for listening to loudspeakers and are therefore usually non-reverberant.

All auditoria have their own resonant characteristics, in that certain frequencies will resonate more than others. Loudspeakers also have resonant characteristics and if the two should coincide, doubly accentuating a certain frequency, the result can be disastrous. In this instance 'room equalization' is a possible cure and is discussed later in the chapter.

SOUND REINFORCEMENT OR PUBLIC ADDRESS

A good sound reinforcement system is conspicuous by its apparent absence. The aim is not to be conscious of a loudspeaker but simply to be able to hear. The job of the sound engineer is therefore to design and instal a reinforcement system which will provide the maximum amount of intelligibility and naturalness while, at the same time, being as unobtrusive as possible.

Conversely, the obvious microphone styles and the sound achieved by cabaret artistes and pop singers cannot be classed as sound reinforcement so much as high quality public address. In the theatre *Hair* and *Jesus Christ Superstar* required the best techniques of P.A. whereas traditional productions like *Fiddler on the Roof* and *Cabaret* called for the more subtle approach of reinforcement.

The requirements of many modern musicals have created a difficult in-between stage. No longer does the soloist always take downstage-centre. And many orchestrations and choral accompaniments are written more for the recording studio than for the theatre. Sometimes the orchestra is even up on stage with the actors, instead of being in the pit. Acting styles have also changed. The musical was the last bastion of declamatory acting, when the 'cue for song' could be seen coming half a page away. Nowadays the cast's ability to sing is often secondary to their ability to act.

Along with these changes there has been perhaps an even greater change in the audience. People no longer visit the theatre prepared to listen. The cinema, radio and television all provide a high level of sound which can be heard without any conscious effort. Another effect of television on the theatre audience is to make them restless. If the happenings on stage fail to grip completely, they no longer feel compelled to sit still and remain quiet. In other words, becoming used to watching television has broken the polite habit of meeting the actor half way.

One way of retaining the attention of an audience is to provide a level of sound it cannot ignore. With a P.A. system this is no problem but with a reinforcement system using long-range microphone techniques it can be extremely difficult.

LOUDSPEAKER PLACEMENT

For a reinforcement system the positioning and angling of loudspeakers is critical. Basic requirements are as follows:

1 They should be positioned as near to the stage as possible to maintain the illusion of the sound coming from the actors.

2 They should be on the audience side of the microphones to minimize acoustic feedback.

3 They should be angled to provide direct sound to every seat in the house.

Multiple loudspeaker installations It is possible to place loudspeakers overhead or round the walls of an auditorium but unless a sophisticated electronic delay system is incorporated the various time lags involved will provide a confusing multiple and disembodied sound. One would first hear the nearest loudspeaker, then progressively distant ones, and finally the original live source. A multiple system is only used under extremely difficult acoustic or architectural conditions. The delay system is normally so calculated that air-borne sound from the stage area arrives at each loudspeaker a fraction of a second before the electronic sound. The effect then is similar to that of direct sound being reinforced naturally by reflecting off an acoustically designed ceiling. Unfortunately an efficient delay system is a very sophisticated piece of electronic equipment which comes at a correspondingly high price.

Line source column loudspeakers A line source column speaker is reasonably small and neat in appearance and has a clearly defined directivity pattern designed for reinforcement. As such, it is the basis of most installations.

Repeating what has already been said in Chapter 3, a good line source speaker is characterized by a wide, smooth frequency range with minimum colouration of sound and, most importantly, a directional coverage which is wide in the horizontal plane and narrow in the vertical. A Bozak column I have used with great success incorporates six 6 in. (150 mm) speakers for the lower frequencies and a row of twelve 2 in. (50 mm) units for the high. This produces a coverage which is 60 degrees horizontal and only 25 degrees vertical. The frequency range of this, and indeed most reinforcement columns, is such that for high quality music reproduction it is necessary to add bass supplement loudspeakers, in separate larger cabinets.

The ideal listening position for a loudspeaker would be slap bang in the middle of the stage, as in a cinema. But as this is hardly practical a compromise has to be found. Remembering that the ears are less discerning in the vertical plane as opposed to the horizontal, the obvious alternative position would be directly above the front of the stage. And this, indeed, is to be recommended in many circumstances. The usual drawback is the sightline cut-off from

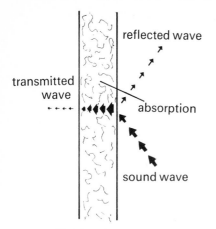

Fig 97 *Reflection
(the angle of incidence
of the sound wave equals
the angle of reflection),
absorption and
transmission.*

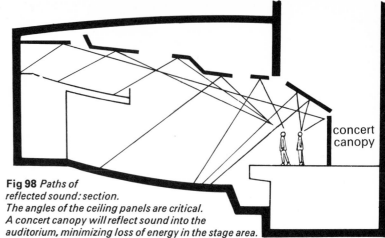

Fig 98 *Paths of
reflected sound: section.
The angles of the ceiling panels are critical.
A concert canopy will reflect sound into the
auditorium, minimizing loss of energy in the stage area.*

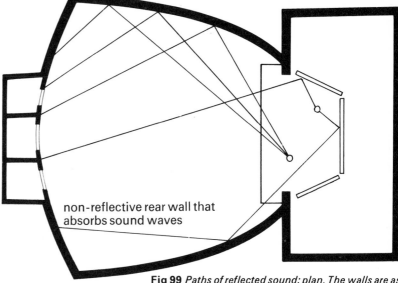

Fig 99 *Paths of reflected sound: plan. The walls are as
important as the ceiling.*

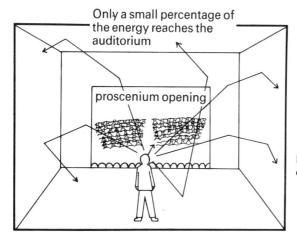

Fig 100 *Reflections and wastage
of energy within an empty stage*

overhanging balconies. If there are seats in the house where it is not possible to see the top of the proscenium arch then direct sound will not reach those seats from loudspeakers placed in that position.

However, successful use was made of this technique for *The Rocky Horror Show*, which had been playing for a number of months in a London cinema under sentence of demolition. When the bulldozers finally approached it was decided to move the show to another disused cinema. Everything was successfully transferred except for the sound quality. Not a word could be understood. Tests in the auditorium showed a general unpleasant accentuation at certain frequencies and a particularly nasty 'flutter echo'. This is the kind of multiple reverberation which produces rapid echoes like a bird fluttering away when you clap your hands.

There were no sightline problems so I decided to do away with the conventional loudspeakers at each side of the proscenium, replacing them by one central group overhead. The main reason was to cut down the number of sources of sound, thereby respectively reducing the causes of echoes. The secondary reason was that the slim restricted power and frequency range columns could be replaced by some beefy bass cabinets and horns more suited to a rock show. The result was a great improvement.

Height Returning to the columns at each side of the stage, it is important to position them as low down as possible. If they are essentially in the same plane and as close to the original source as feasible not only will the angle of coverage be correct but there will be minimum source identification.

My rule of thumb is to sit in the back row and have the loudspeaker set down to a position where I can just see the entire unit above the head of a person in the row in front.

Direction They should be swivelled so that imaginary lines from the centre of each pair of columns would not quite meet. Loudspeakers are only mounted in a cross-fire positions if architectural features preclude all else.

Blasting the front rows Some people imagine that the front few rows of the stalls will now be blasted out, but if the loudspeaker is angled correctly this will not be the case. If you are near to and slightly below it you will receive the benefit of only a small part of the total energy.

As you retreat you come more and more into range until you reach a point where you are directly receiving the entire output of the loudspeaker.

It is exactly like light. One person can sit near a spotlight under the beam and be lit by a general glow while another person farther back has the light focused full upon him. Therefore it is essential to tilt the loudspeaker so that the maximum amount of sound reaches the rear of the auditorium. In order not to starve the front and centre sections I usually aim about three rows down from the back.

Aiming It is not possible to aim a column loudspeaker accurately by eye. There is, however, a simple method which requires two people, a torch and a mirror. Attach a small mirror to the centre of the front of the column. From the desired position aim a torch at eye level into the mirror. Then tilt the column until the reflection of the torch is visible in the mirror.

I usually prefer to make final adjustments by ear. The requisites for this operation are two people (one with a good pair of ears) and some hiss. By turning up a few empty channels on the mixer with plenty of mid and treble added, it is usually possible to obtain a reasonable hiss level. The person with the good ears, moving around the auditorium, will quickly discover where the signal is strongest and where it drops away. The point at which the two beams cross is also very striking and should, naturally, be in the centre of the auditorium. By swaying from side to side in this position one is extremely aware of moving from one loudspeaker to the other. If they are wired out of phase then the sensation will be most unpleasant, and the fault should be remedied immediately.

It is important to remember that the audience are seated. Therefore if the angles are correct for the back row the hiss will drop away sharply as you stand. The reverse will be true for the front few rows for the reasons already discussed (i.e. not 'blasting' the front rows).

If there is a loud orchestra in the pit the audience near the stage may require considerable assistance from the sound system. This is always a tricky problem. A quick, though not always effective, solution is to compromise on the requirements at front and back and aim somewhere in between, at the same time angling the speakers inwards a little more. The best way of filling in the dead triangle at the front of the stalls is by adding more loudspeakers. Two columns angled as necessary will do the trick. Or it is sometimes possible to mount a column or horn loudspeaker directly above the centre of the proscenium. It will be necessary to adjust the signal strength of these 'fill-in' units carefully, so that they not only blend in with the overall system but they do not cause feedback.

I find that it is a great help to cup both hands behind the ears when concentrating on hiss levels. I recently discovered that my colleagues, well used to seeing me running up and down the aisles with hands behind the ears and an intent expression upon the face, now standing, now crouching and generally bobbing about from side to side, have christened the operation 'Doing Rabbits'.

CONTROL EQUIPMENT

AMPLIFIERS

Usually one amplifier for each pair of loudspeakers will give the required flexibility for 'balancing' between each floor of the auditorium. Acoustic conditions will often make it necessary to drive the dress circle (first balcony) loudspeakers as hard as possible while the amplifiers associated with the stalls and upper circle can be attenuated to provide a similar listening condition.

If the system is in stereo then one amplifier per loudspeaker will be required. Speech reinforcement is not usually attempted in stereo for one good basic reason: it can only work if the loudspeaker coverage from each side embraces the entire auditorium. This can be achieved from an overhead position but is hardly worth attempting from the side. That being said, stereo may be required in a system which also incorporates live music reinforcement and/or tape playback.

MIXERS

With a complicated multi-microphone set-up it is an advantage to have equalization (tone controls) individually on every input channel. Some of the channels should accept line level outputs from tape decks, ancillary mixers, etc.

The most flexible arrangement is to have each channel switchable microphone/line.

In a stereo situation pan controls associated with the two output groups will be required on each channel. Ecno or reverberation facilities are a very useful adjunct.

It is most convenient if instead of there being only two output sockets for the mixer (left and right) there are a number of paralleled sockets. This will enable a quantity of amplifiers to be fed direct without having to go via an additional plug box arrangement. In the interests of trouble-free operation floating leads and connections should be kept to a minimum.

On a mixer I once had built for a show there was incorporated an added luxury which turned out to be almost an essential. At the output end of the mixer after the main group faders were four pairs of output sockets. Associated with each pair were separate gain, bass, mid and treble controls. This meant that when the stereo pairs of amplifiers were connected for the four floors of the auditorium one could not only adjust the gain for each floor, but one could change the equalization. Thus, whereas the stalls required a little bass cut because the 'float' ('foot' or 'apron' in the US) microphones tended to feed back at that frequency, the circle required a mid-lift, and the gallery, being a great distance away from the speakers, required a hefty boost of mid and top.

LIMITERS AND COMPRESSORS

There are devices, originally designed for recording studios, which can electronically control sound levels. A limiter can be set so that extremely strong signals which might cause amplifier overloading and distortion are automatically reduced. In other words, one can set a ceiling on the peaks. However, a word of warning, the limiter must be of extremely good quality and design, and must even then not be overdriven, otherwise the unit itself will introduce distortion.

A limiter/compressor is a device which not only limits the peaks but boosts the smaller signals. So all the signals become compressed between a predetermined floor and ceiling. This is a tricky piece of equipment to use with live amplification as it is very prone to pulling the signal up into feedback.

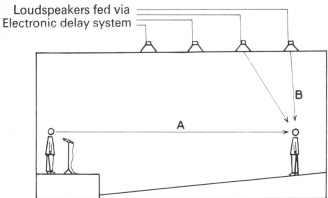

Fig 101 *Distributed loudspeaker system. The live sound A should reach the listener a fraction of a second before the reinforced sound B. Hence a delay system is required.*

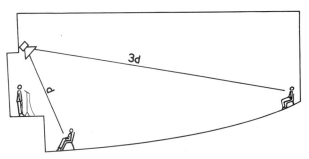

Fig 102 *Ceiling speakers in a criss-cross pattern with 50 per cent overlap*

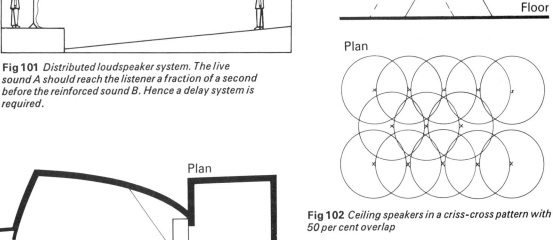

Plan

2 horn loudspeakers

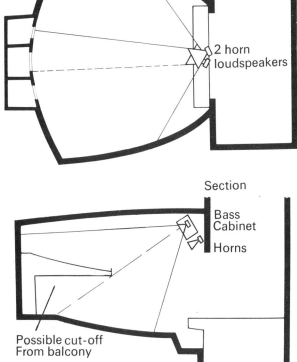

Section

Bass Cabinet

Horns

Possible cut-off From balcony

Fig 103 *A single loudspeaker complex placed centrally above the proscenium will minimize multiple reflections and time lags.*

Fig 104 *The most remote location covered by an overhead loudspeaker (3d) should not normally be more than three times the distance of the nearest location (d).*

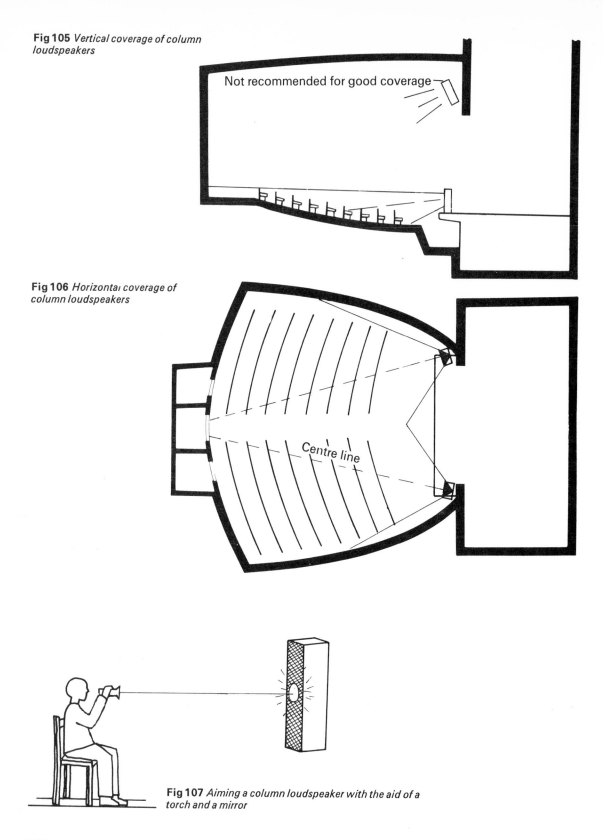

Fig 105 *Vertical coverage of column loudspeakers*

Not recommended for good coverage

Fig 106 *Horizontal coverage of column loudspeakers*

Centre line

Fig 107 *Aiming a column loudspeaker with the aid of a torch and a mirror*

ANTI-FEEDBACK DEVICES

Acoustic feedback or howlround is caused by the signal from a loudspeaker being picked up by a microphone, going round through the system and out of the loudspeaker again ad infinitum.

The beginnings of feedback are characterized by a zing on the end of each word. Unless the microphone level is checked this builds into what is called a ringing sound. And this, in turn, will build into a howl or scream.

The frequency of the feedback tone will depend upon many factors. These include the characteristics of the microphone and the loudspeaker, the resonant characteristics of the environment and the position of the microphone in relation to the loudspeaker; for example, the feedback tone produced with a microphone behind a loudspeaker will tend to be of a low frequency in contrast with the high notes produced in front.

Audio experts are constantly researching new ideas for obtaining a dramatic increase in gain before feedback and there are some devices now on the market which certainly help towards that aim. One such unit is called a phase inverter and it is based on the principle that feedback builds up as the cones of the loudspeakers oscillate at a certain frequency and with a gathering momentum. The phase inverter will, at regular intervals, completely reverse the polarity or phasing of all the loudspeakers. This checks the momentum by sending a positive impulse when the loudspeaker is expecting to receive a negative one. After a pause the feedback will begin to build up again and the process is repeated. I have experienced about a 4 dB gain under performance conditions, which is fairly considerable.

Room equalization There is a growing tendency, particularly with permanent installations, to advocate 'room voicing'. With this process the environment is first tested electronically to discover its resonant characteristics and all the frequencies which are accentuated are carefully plotted on a graph. The sound system is then equalized to suit the room. This is achieved by introducing a broadband passive equalizer which incorporates a series of filters with passbands of a third octave or narrower. By adjusting these filters it is possible to iron out the peaks previously plotted on the graph.

This bending of the frequency pattern of the sound equipment will not only make the sound seem to be of better quality but will drastically reduce feedback problems.

'Normalizing' a sound system to a room properly is a complicated business but it can produce dramatic results.

MICROPHONES

In a reinforcement system where the requirement is for maximum distant pick-up with minimum feedback potential we are dealing almost exclusively with directional or cardioid microphones. Some examples of exceptions to this rule will be given later when specific shows are discussed.

It might reasonably be conjectured that the more microphones there are scattered about a stage the better will be the general coverage. This is unfortunately not the case. The rule is to use as few microphones as possible.

When more than one microphone is brought up on the mixer the potential acoustic gain is reduced. In fact, each time the number of open microphones is doubled it has been calculated that 3 dB of gain-before-feedback is lost.

Another reason for economy is that the greater the number of microphones the less clean will be the sound. Reflections, reverberations and time-lags will create a very unpleasant and 'mikey' sound.

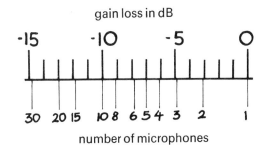

Fig 108 *Gain loss in dB using multiple microphones*

Positioning and mounting The object is to get the microphones in front of and as near to the original source of sound as possible. This may be achieved by placing them either at floor level or raised up on stands along the front edge of the stage, suspending them from above, or hiding them within the scenic element.

It is pointless suspending microphones downstage at a normal border height of 20 feet (6 m) or so. The actors will be delivering their lines forwards and not upwards. And the front-stage microphone position will at most times be nearer to the actor anyhow.

Suspension from above is useful farther upstage if no better solution presents itself. In this instance a very directional 'gun' microphone would be advocated. The gun should be positioned slightly in front of the desired pick-up area, pointing downwards but tilted slightly upstage. Because of the general ambient noise always picked up by a long range microphone it is advisable to install these sparingly and to use them throughout a performance only when strictly necessary.

Overhead suspension is also useful for picking up actors on staircases, rostra, etc. A good quality normal cardioid might be better than a gun if the distance above the actor's heads is no more than about 8 feet (2·5 m).

It is very tempting to use a convenient lighting bar for this purpose. But remember the possibility of induced interference from electrical cables, especially when associated with electronic lighting dimmers. If it is not possible to keep clear altogether, the microphone cables should at least be run from the opposite end of the bar to the mains cables.

The favourite position for the first line of reinforcement is along the front edge of the stage. This is an obvious choice, being directly in the firing line between the actors and the audience. Traditionally this is the position of the old 'footlights' or 'floats', so called because they were once lighted wicks floating in wax. So, in the UK, we tend to refer to them as 'float microphones' or, for short, 'floats'.

Fig 109 *Makeshift shock-absorbent mounting for a float microphone*

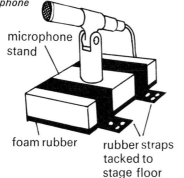

microphone stand

foam rubber

rubber straps tacked to stage floor

Some form of rubber shock absorbent mounting is essential for float microphones as they are very susceptible to transmitted vibrations. Any shock to the stage floor, like a footfall or a heavy scenery truck being moved, will cause the structure to vibrate, and the vibrations will be transmitted to any solidly fixed microphone, causing unpleasant bass frequency sounds.

Unwanted air-borne sounds of footfalls and scenic movement are another matter. They will, of course, be picked up by the microphones in direct ratio to the wanted speech. But the remedy here relies more on rubber soled shoes and a disciplined stage crew than microphone technique.

If no adequate shock mounts are available (and there are very few on the market which are small or efficient enough) there is an easy makeshift solution. Place the stand on a piece of half-inch (13 mm) or thicker foam rubber and make the whole thing secure with strips of real rubber over the stand base tacked to the floor at either side.

A completely different approach is to stand or fix the microphone on to some solid surface which has no direct contact with the stage floor, perhaps the floor of the auditorium, or clamped to the brick wall at the rear of the orchestra pit.

Height of float microphones It was once the object of every sound man to raise the float microphones as near as possible to the height of the source of sound, that is, an actor's head. And many arguments have ensued with set designers, producers and directors *vis-à-vis* their unsightliness as opposed to the importance of audibility (photograph 38).

Where a stage floor is carpeted or covered with some non-reflective material microphones are still often required to be at a height of 3 feet (1 m) or so. Some manufacturers cater for this with extremely thin extension tubes for condenser microphones which fit between the capsule and the body.

However, where a stage floor has a hard reflective surface a different technique is used. It was once discovered when some sound engineers were testing out a very large installation in America that one of the microphones appeared to be very much more efficient than all the others. The range of pick-up was better

102

and the clarity was improved. Upon closer inspection they were surprised to find that the microphone in question had fallen from its stand and was resting on the floor. Later tests with sophisticated electronic equipment proved the validity of their initial findings.

When a microphone is raised off the ground it will receive direct sounds and reflected sounds. Some of the reflections will arrive at the microphone out of phase, and cancel out certain groups of frequencies. If the microphone is placed at floor level these cancellations cannot occur, and the tonal balance will be similar to a close microphone technique.

Shure (in the USA) manufacture a special 'Distant Pick-up' isolation stand for their cardioid microphones and Theatre Projects (in the UK) manufacture a foam-rubber mount made for use with an AKG condenser microphone which incorporates a swivel adaptor to angle the capsule. Because they are long, low and grey we have called these 'mice'.

To be effective the stand must support the microphone as close to the floor as possible with the business end about $\frac{1}{8}$ in. (3 mm) away from it. The angle should be between 30 and 45 degrees.

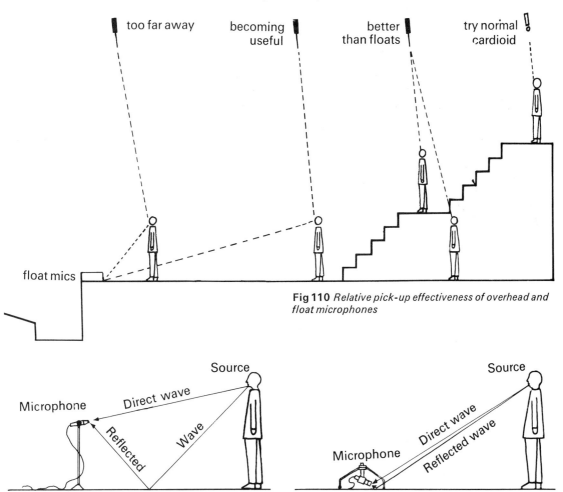

overhead gun microphones

too far away   becoming useful   better than floats   try normal cardioid

float mics

Fig 110 *Relative pick-up effectiveness of overhead and float microphones*

Fig 111 *Direct and reflected waves reaching a microphone on a high stand will be out of phase, thereby cancelling out certain frequencies.*

103

Transmitted foot noise will be catered for by correct shock isolation, and air-borne foot noise will not noticeably increase. Footfalls 6 feet (2 m) away will be picked up similarly whether the microphone is at floor level or a foot or two in the air.

An added bonus is that the stage floor not only acts as a collector of sound waves but it tends to shield the microphone from the orchestra pit and the loudspeakers. Therefore a higher level before feedback may be obtained with less pick-up from an orchestra.

Spacing of float microphones For an even coverage float microphones should be set on about 5 foot (1·5 m) centres. They should certainly not be spaced more than 6 feet (2 m) apart.

Radio microphones If an important solo artiste in a musical cannot be heard it is not necessarily the fault of the reinforcement system. It might be a combination of many factors: overheavy orchestrations, acoustically unsympathetic stage setting, lack of available good· microphone positions, untrained singing voice or excessive choreography, producing a breathless actor who may sometimes be facing away from the microphones.

The simple way out when faced with this situation is to give the actor a radiomicrophone. The kit comes in two or three parts, the microphone and transmitter, which can be separate or integrated, and the receiver. The receiver with its aerial (or antenna) simply plugs into an input on the mixer like an ordinary microphone. The transmitter pack, tuned to the same frequency as the receiver, is secreted somewhere in the actor's clothing. The associated microphone is hung round the neck on a lavalier cord or, better still, fixed in a specially made pocket, setting the head of the microphone in a central chest position, approximately 4 in. (100 mm) below the chin.

The microphone will be of the omnidirectional variety, providing a general pick-up to cope with all the head movements. Since it is so near the source of sound there are unlikely to be serious feedback problems. There will, however, be unwanted pick-up problems when an actor wearing a radiomicrophone comes into range of one who is not. Here the skill of the sound operator will tell in deft yet subtle adjustments of gain.

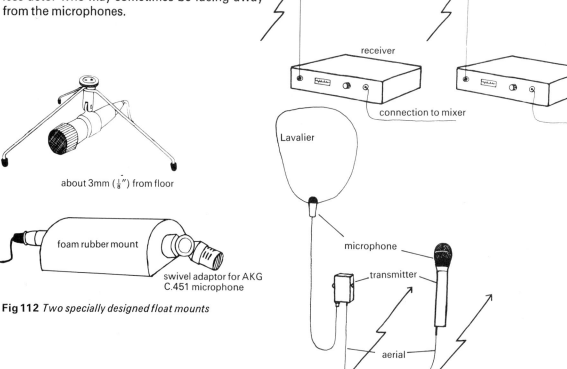

Fig 112 *Two specially designed float mounts*

about 3mm ($\frac{1}{8}$") from floor

foam rubber mount

swivel adaptor for AKG C.451 microphone

aerial

receiver

connection to mixer

Lavalier

microphone

transmitter

aerial

Lavalier   Hand-held

Fig 113 *Radiomicrophone systems*

A radio is least obvious to the audience when it is used only as a gentle aid to the general reinforcement system. It is seldom necessary to use it for dialogue unless heavily underscored.

Some of the drawbacks and pitfalls are:

1 They are susceptible to interference from static electricity if worn under clothes made of silk, etc.

2 The short aerials on the transmitters can cause trouble if they get crumpled up in the clothing or, worse still, broken. This important little piece of wire must be kept relatively straight. It can well be stuck to the skin with a piece of sticking plaster.

3 They can sound muffled if the head of the microphone is not either completely free or covered by only a thin material.

4 Unless the microphone is firmly fixed there is the danger that it may rustle against clothing.

5 There is always the possibility of interference from other radio equipment in the vicinity. (I once experienced a great deal of unpleasant noise on a system at the Theatre Royal, Drury Lane, London, the cause of which turned out to be a mobile X-ray unit parked outside.)

6 In Great Britain where the GPO exercise a strict control over radio frequencies, the number of microphones it is safe to use within the band of allotted frequencies is limited. Each microphone operates on its own frequency, and when dealing with quantities in excess of four or five there is the ever-present danger of interaction.

7 In America, where the licensing laws are a little more lax there is always the possibility of a radio paging system for a hotel or taxi service in the vicinity sharing your frequency.

One of my favourite radiomicrophone anecdotes arose from the rehearsals of *Joseph and the Amazing Technicolour Dreamcoat* which was in a theatre backing on to where *Godspell* was playing. In *Joseph* we actually had six radiomicrophones, so were using up most of the frequencies available.

In the middle of our first sound rehearsal there suddenly appeared beside the mixing desk a breathless and ashen-faced stage manager from the theatre next door. Apparently Joseph's voice was being picked up on the *Godspell*

system. Although I pointed out that a touch of Old Testament might not be out of place in his show, he failed to see the humour of the situation and we were forced to change to another radio frequency.

Riser microphones Although microphones rising out of the stage floor are no longer in fashion they are sometimes required, especially for cabaret and night-club work. They can be mechanically operated by means of a hand-winch or an electric motor. The more sophisticated motorized risers can be made to stop at any height and they will also disappear smoothly and silently through the stage floor, closing the trap afterwards. With any riser it is essential to mute the microphone while the mechanism is in operation.

SETTING OPTIMUM LEVELS

Once the system is installed to our satisfaction we set about the business of discovering exactly how much the equipment will do for us. During rehearsals a great number of minor adjustments will necessarily be carried out as deficiencies become apparent. But a starting point must be found.

This is one method of tackling the problem. Switch on the amplifier or amplifiers driving the circle (first balcony) loudspeakers and set their main gain at a point off maximum. This is because the stalls will probably require less gain but the upper circle could well need more. Next fade up the centre float microphone until it starts to feed back. It should now be so contrived that this feedback point occurs only when the fader is fully open, either by adjusting the channel 'sensitivity' ('harsh gain' control) or, with a less sophisticated system, by adjusting the amplifiers themselves.

A further adjustment is now necessary to make the system completely stable even when someone is shouting and stamping around in front of the microphone. This achieved, a central reference is obtained around which the rest of the system can be set.

The other amplifiers are introduced until they are all at maximum level before feedback. Then with the centre float microphone taken down about 5 dB (or one point if the mixer is not scaled in decibels of attenuation) the rest of the floats are brought in. A certain amount of juggling with levels will probably be necessary as the various microphone positions will cause feedback in different loudspeakers and at varying frequencies.

Finally, a thorough listening test should be carried out. With an assistant on stage speaking at a constant level all parts of the theatre should be visited. It might be found that the acoustics on one floor are so good that the relative amplifiers can be reduced in gain. This will improve the stability of the system and provide a little in hand for boosting another section of the auditorium.

Before the first sound rehearsal with the

Fig 114 *Diagram of rig for* Company

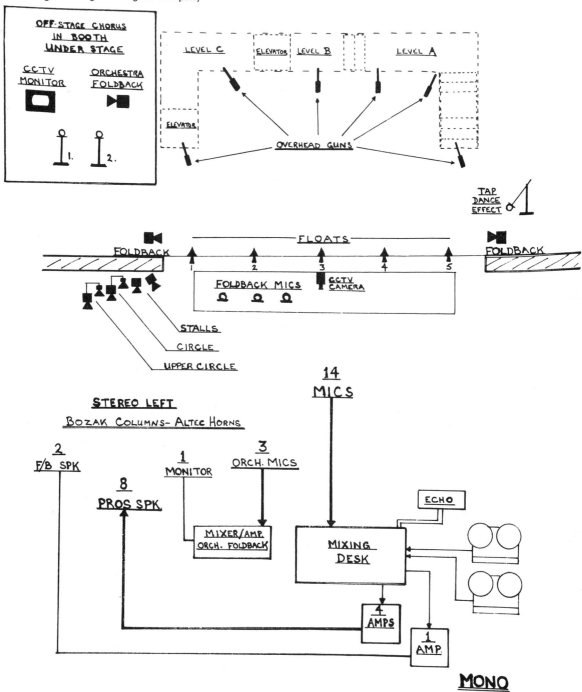

actors all the other microphones should be tested for maximum levels. The areas of effective pick up must also be checked, and re-positioning carried out as necessary.

Assuming that all ancillary equipment, like tape machines, reverberation, etc., has been checked we are now ready to meet the actors.

The following are interesting examples of problems encountered on various productions.

Company This musical (with music and lyrics by Stephen Sondheim) was first produced on Broadway in 1970 and later transferred to London. It was, incidentally, the first time an entire American show — cast, sets, costumes and all — was air-lifted across the Atlantic. Only the sound and lighting equipment were English.

As the cast were scheduled to arrive only three days before the first public preview, leaving very little time for technical experimentation, I flew to New York to prime myself with the problems before they arrived.

Jack Mann, the American sound expert, had carried out an extremely impressive job on a very tricky show. And I was able to benefit not only by his intimate knowledge of the production but by the very good rig which he had evolved during the pre-Broadway tour.

The orchestra was large, twenty-four, for a small cast musical and included two electric guitars and an electric organ. Experience has shown that 200 watts or so of sound under the control of three musicians usually makes for headaches (in every sense of the word). The volume levels tend to creep up during a period of performances with the rest of the orchestra trying to compete. And the smallest adjustment of a guitar amplifier can completely obliterate a carefully worked out sound balance.

It is essential therefore that the sound man has a good working relationship with an understanding musical director. And we were fortunate enough on that show to have one of the best. Hal Hastings used to say that he had a method of judging the balance of his orchestra to the stage, and it went like this : 'I reckon it is my job to control the orchestra so that from my position in the front of the pit I can hear all the lyrics from the stage. After that it is up to the sound man.' Nothing could be fairer than that.

The lyrics in the case of *Company* were very important yet often very difficult to get across. Even on the cast album the complex orchestra-tions and vocal arrangements make it hard to discern certain passages. On stage we had the added complication of a large open skeletal set on several levels with very few microphone positions near enough to the singers to be suitable for the precise pick-up required.

An example of the kind of problem encountered was for the number 'Someone is Waiting'. The leading man starts singing stage centre then walks to a staircase stage left which transports him, still singing, to a 7 foot (2·1 m) level. Moving stage right he now reaches a motor-driven elevator which takes him to a higher level, then on to some more stairs leading down to a second elevator which drops him back to stage level for the final note of the song.

Throughout the number a fairly heavy orchestration was augmented by an off-stage chorus (on echo). And at certain points during the number other members of the cast, widely dispersed around the set, also had to join in.

Single float microphones were used for the beginning and end with a series of gun microphones for the movement around the various levels. The sound operator literally followed the leading man around the set so that at no time were there more than two microphones live for this purpose. The pick-up of the other people on the set was from the nearest float or gun ; but strictly on cue as necessary. In this way a 'tight' sound was maintained. The off-stage chorus, watching the musical director via closed-circuit television, posed no problems of feedback, being well out of the way. But they did pose a problem of balance and clarity. Originally the two microphones for the five singers were positioned in the wings where they could both hear the orchestra and see the conductor. But as many of the backing vocals occurred during scene changes an alternative position had to be found. Under stage was first tried with the door to the orchestra pit propped open to obtain a view of the conductor. Unfortunately, the microphones picked up the drum kit and brass section almost as much as the singers. So the door had to be closed and the microphones moved to a quieter corner of the understage area. The brick walls and concrete floor created very unpleasant acoustics, so a carpet was laid and heavy drapes hung around the walls. The microphones were omnidirectional and moun-ted on high stands with one for the ladies and one for the gentlemen.

The gun microphones on stage were on brackets fixed to overhead lighting bars. Each was positioned about 3 feet (1 m) downstage of the required area of pick-up, pointing roughly at the feet of the singer. A great deal of experimentation with tone controls was carried out to equalize the guns to the better quality float microphones.

There was one joke effect of a purposely over-amplified tap dance. In this particular number there were short breaks for single members of the cast to perform short tap solos. The director wanted to overdo the whole thing and bring the floats way up. However, this did not have the required effect. So instead the float mikes were killed completely and we had a dancer off stage tapping away on a suitably hard surface some twelve inches (300 mm) away from a directional microphone. The result was extremely comic.

Another interesting effect was achieved when the cast were called upon to sustain a very long note while moving rapidly about the entire set. Not only did they run out of breath but the microphone coverage could not be that good. The problem was solved by recording the note so that the tape could take over as the live voices faded. The sound operator coped with the transition so well that even I could never tell where it happened.

Pippin and *The Good Companions* For these productions, both in the same theatre as *Company*, we added microphones in the orchestra pit, not necessarily to make it louder, but to give the composers and orchestrators the balance and presence they required. A string or woodwind section will sound very dead in most orchestra pits and a harp, string bass or piano will often not be heard at all. So some subtle reinforcement with very directional microphones placed as near to the instruments as possible can compensate. However, it is not good enough to leave all these microphones open at set levels throughout an entire show. A balance must be found for each musical item. There will be occasions when certain microphones must be killed because they are, for example, picking up and over amplifying a loud brass passage.

For operational reasons it is a good plan to use a sub-mixer for the orchestra. The internal balance can then be preset and brought up on cue with a master fader. It also gives scope for general variations in level during the number.

There is an old lighting trick of fading up that extra bit of light for the end of each song. This is to give a lift which will encourage applause. A similar lift may be obtained with the judicious use of the orchestra master fader.

Billy at the Theatre Royal, Drury Lane, London, was one of the biggest headaches of all, having an enormous permanent box set made of steel clad in hardboard. Drury Lane is one of London's largest theatres and the set itself was 4 feet (1·2 m) deeper from footlights to back wall than the largest stage on Broadway. From the point of view of acoustics, it was like working on a completely empty reverberant stage. A close microphone technique seemed to be called for, but where to place them?

Gun microphones were of no use because of the height. Most of the staircases and platforms were flat steel motorized units with nowhere to hide anything. The one conventional piece of scenery, a two storey cut-away house on a truck, was seized upon and microphones were set behind the television, amongst the tea cups on the table, over the doorway in the hall and beside the wardrobe in the bedroom. A few more positions were found for 'specials', i.e. microphones specifically placed to do a job in perhaps only one song. After that we had to rely on floats and radios.

The star, Michael Crawford, who was on stage for the entire performance apart from speedy costume changes, wore two radio microphones (photograph 39). A great deal of dancing and acrobatics sometimes made for broken aerials (antennae) or intermittent connections, when the standby would immediately be brought into service. Three other characters also used radios, though not for all their numbers. It depended upon the orchestration, the costumes they were wearing and their position on stage relative to the floats.

One of the numbers was completely on tape with the cast miming. This posed no particular problem except for the transition from live to taped sound. A good signal from loudspeakers on stage as well as from the front-of-house system was required otherwise the sound would have appeared to have a hole in it.

Mixed live and taped sound In certain shows, particularly large scale revues, it is necessary or advantageous to have all or part of the vocals prerecorded. Keeping the orchestra synchronized with the tape is the essence of this operation. This is done by recording a separate 'click track' giving a very definite and constant beat for the musical director (and sometimes also the drummer) to hear via a headset. It can be very effective to have a recorded choral arrangement from loudspeakers on stage with the live chorus and soloists also singing. The microphone

Fig 115 *Diagram of rig for* Billy

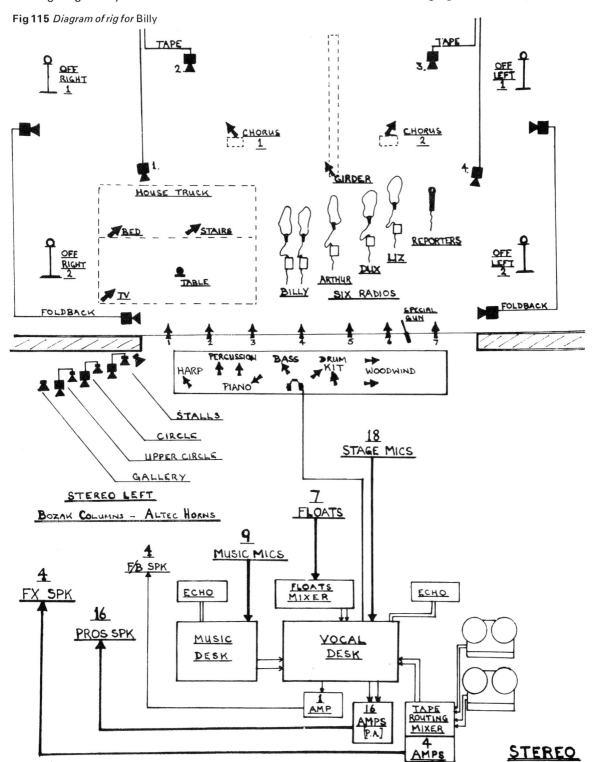

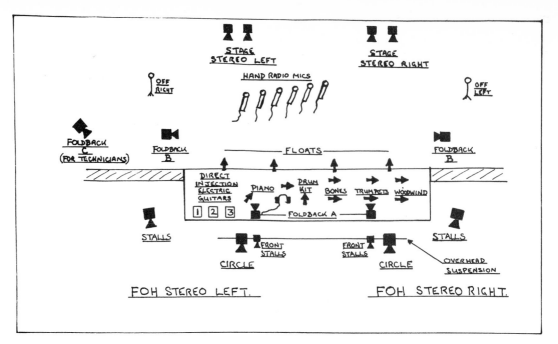

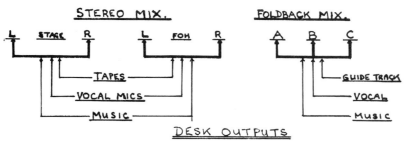

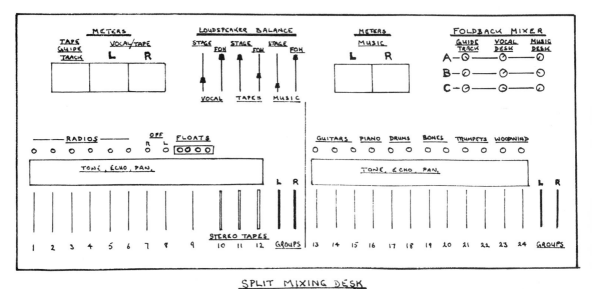

Fig 116 *System for microphone/tape show in stereo as installed at the Royalty Theatre, London, in 1974. The desk has three stereo outputs (tape, vocal microphones and music microphones) which are mixed as required to stage loudspeakers and auditorium loudspeakers. There are three foldback outputs which are premixes of the vocal desk (including tape), the music desk and the conductor's guide track which is on the third track of the tape.*

Fig 117 *Rig for* Jesus Christ Superstar

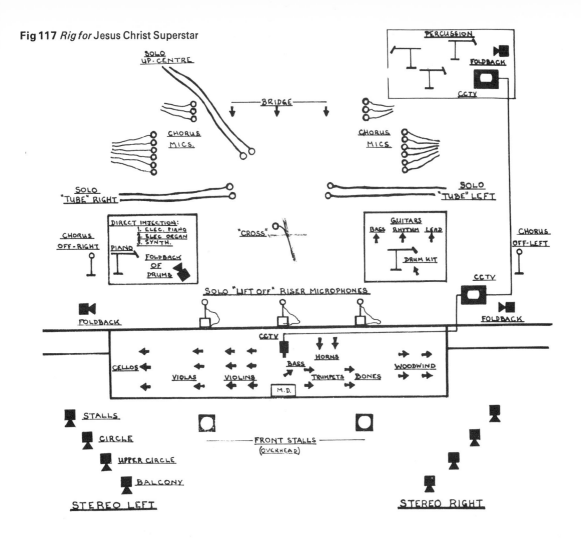

Fig 118 Jesus Christ Superstar. *Layout of mixing desk showing sub-grouping and channels using limiter/compressors.*

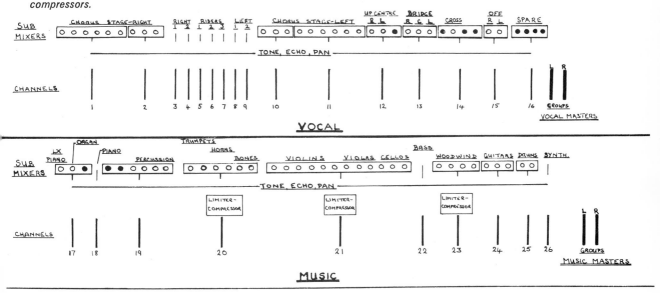

system picks everything up and blends it into a whole.

Jesus Christ Superstar The London production came after the American, the Australian and several European versions. Originally a record album, it was turned into a show with varying degrees of success in different countries. Jim Sharman, who directed an ambitious stage production and a static concert version in Australia, was asked to direct it in England. The musical director, Anthony Bowles, had worked on the Paris production. And they were agreed that musically the concert versions worked best.

They determined, therefore, to produce the show on a set which precluded a great deal of movement and to use a close microphone technique throughout. Even the chorus whenever possible would be on individual hand microphones. With a multi-microphone installation for the orchestra as well it should be possible to obtain a recording studio type of balance.

The problem of the distribution of microphones was resolved by having downstage in the floats three riser microphones which could be lifted off for hand use, plus six other hand microphones (colour coded for easy identification) situated around the stage. Three general pick-up microphones were placed upstage although they were seldom used. There were eighteen hand microphones for chorus use distributed around the upper levels of the set plus two for off-stage choruses (photograph 40).

We had a lot of trouble in the final scene trying to pick up the actor playing Jesus when he was suspended on the crucifix. Eventually a small black omnidirectional microphone attached to a strip of metal was fixed to the cross so that it stuck out somewhere above his right shoulder. A bass cut and mid lift at the mixing desk compensated for the fact that he was 'off-mike'.

The thirty musicians were split up with the main orchestra in the pit, the rock group in two sections either side of the acting area on stage, and an overspill percussion section in a separate space off-stage. In all thirty-three directional microphones were used for the orchestra plus a direct feed into a line input channel from the synthesizer. With the vocal microphones the grand total amounted to sixty-seven channels.

In order to control and balance such a large installation, a special mixing desk was devised.

It was obviously not physically possible to manipulate this number of faders so a certain amount of sub-grouping was incorporated in the design. For example, one channel would control four 'woodwind' microphones. Each microphone had its own preset gain control but one channel fader with equalization, echo, panning, etc. mastered the lot. Certain chorus microphones were also grouped in a similar fashion.

The desk was now reduced to twenty-six main channels, which was still too much for one man to cope with. So the desk was split down the middle into voice and music channels to allow for two operators.

The loudspeakers in the auditorium were eight Altec 'Voice of the Theatre' systems with bass bins and horns, plus two smaller units for front stalls fill-in. All the loudspeakers were separately powered to allow for stereo.

The initial orchestra balancing session was under the control of Michael Moor who is a first class studio recording engineer. With his skill and experience he was able to produce the right sound from each instrument to please the musical director, and blend them into an exciting overall sound. He had the unusual task of not only balancing the orchestra through loudspeakers, as in a normal recording studio, but at the same time making sure that the sound via the speakers enhanced the natural sound of the live orchestra in the auditorium.

In New York they tried covering the pit completely with glass. And the conductor stood in a perspex bubble. This presumably made balancing an easier task but the theatrical and exciting sound of a live orchestra was lost. So the glass had to go.

The musical director was very insistent that *Superstar* should not become for the audience what he termed 'an aural assault course'. The purpose of the sound system was to produce a studio quality balance with the added excitement of a live performance. There are very few places where the music is really loud. But there are many places where just the piano or guitars are backing a quiet solo. The final number in Act One ranges from unaided solo voice with quiet piano to close microphone with full strings, brass, percussion, rock group and all. The proper use and control of this kind of dynamic range made *Jesus Christ Superstar* a unique experience.

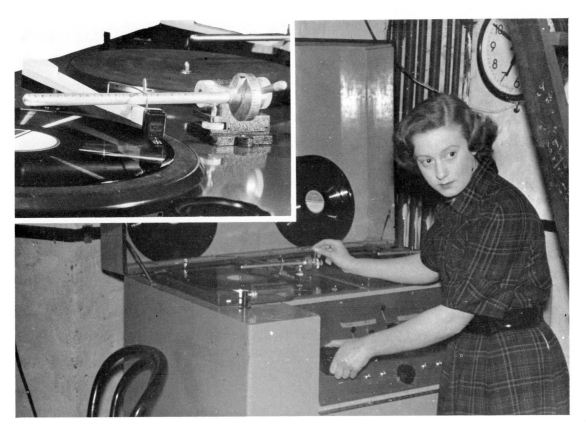

27 *A panatrope in use*
28 *Close up of groove locator and pick-up arm lowering device for a panatrope* (inset)

29 *Taped sound effects at Theatre Royal Drury Lane in 1957*. Photo Courtesy Stagesound (London) Ltd

30 *Professor Lowe recording traffic sounds in Whitehall, London, on a disc-cutting machine (1923).* Inset: *machine for recording the commentaries of BBC reporters in the field during World War II.*

31 *Recording footsteps in the dead of night on tape.
Recording van c. 1960.* Photo Courtesy Stagesound
(London) Ltd

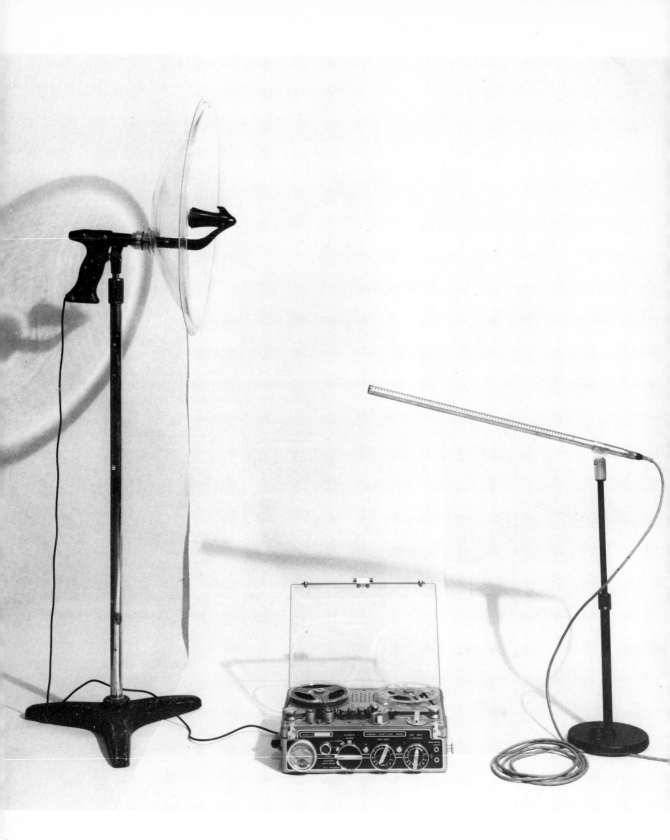

33 *Firing one of the 50 lb cannons of HMS Victory. The recording equipment and engineers are masked by the smoke.* Photo Courtesy Portsmouth and Sunderland Newspapers Ltd

32 *Modern battery/mains professional Nagra tape recorder with Sennheiser gun microphone and Dan Gibson parabolic reflector microphone.*

34 *A section of the 'Trafalgar' exhibit at Madame Tussauds.* Photo Courtesy Madame Tussauds London

35 *One of the stage managers of* Blitz *cueing by radio*

36 *Photographs from* The Sketch *1905 showing the creation of live sound effects.*

37 *A reconstruction of creating the effects backstage for a fifteenth-century mystery play.*

39 *Michael Crawford, star of* Billy *at the Theatre Royal Drury Lane, holds his radio transmitter while sound operator, Claire Laver, adjusts the microphone.*

38 *Photo showing old system of microphones along the front of the stage mounted as high as possible. Note the riser microphone through the trap in the stage floor.*

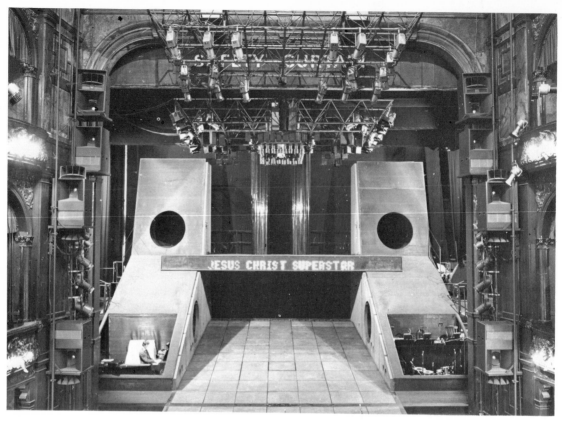

40 Jesus Christ Superstar. *The loudspeakers can clearly be seen around the proscenium. Two speakers placed overhead on the lighting grid cover the front stalls. The three riser microphones are downstage and the chorus hand microphones are distributed around the ramps above the rock group positions.* Photo Courtesy Audio Magazine

41 Jesus Christ Superstar. *Dave Roberts, one of the two sound operators, adjusts one of the foldback amplifiers positioned under stage.* Photo Courtesy Audio Magazine

42 Jesus Christ Superstar. *Roger Norwood controls the vocal end of the eighty-channel Alice mixing desk.* Photo Courtesy Audio Magazine

124

43 *Tape/disc console at Chichester Festival Theatre in 1961*

44 *The author at the Old Vic theatre in 1963 operating the newly installed sound system for the first production of the National Theatre Company of Great Britain,* Hamlet.

45 *Theatr Y Werin: sound mixing desk.* Equipment : Electrosonic Ltd. Photo Courtesy Theatre Projects Consultants Ltd

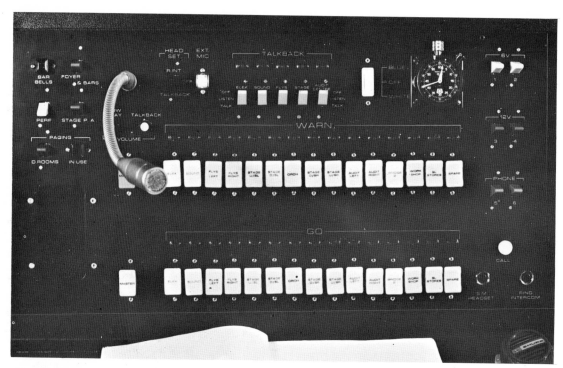

46 *Theatr Y Werin: stage manager's control.* Equipment : Electrosonic Ltd. Photo Courtesy Theatre Projects Consultants Ltd

47 *National Theatre of Great Britain: stage manager's control.* Photo Courtesy Pye Business Communications Ltd

1 SM Ring Volume
2 SM Ring Telephone Call Lights
3 SM Ring Loudspeaker
4 Working Lights and Rehearsal/ Performance Control
5 Technical Ring Loudspeaker
6 Low Voltage Effects Circuits
7 Stop Clock
8 Foyer Paging, Bar Bells and Foyer CCTV 3 minute Performance Warn Sequence
9 Panel Lights and CCTV Source Select
10 CCTV Monitor
11 Ring Intercom Controls
12 House Tabs
13 SM Ring Cueing Control
14 Master Cuelights
15 Microphone
16 Removeable Blue/White Light Unit
17 PA to Stage
18 Paging Artists/Technicians
19 Headset/Hand Mic. Switches
20 Talkback Loudspeaker
21 Talkback Volume
22 Talkback Circuits
23 Pabx External Telephone
24 Cuelights
25 SM Ring Telephone
26 Extension Cuelight 'GO' Circuits

48 *National Theatre of Great Britain: general facilities panel. A triple compartment metal box with section one for mains, section two for low level signals and section three for high level signals. An extendable cuelight unit may be plugged in at the top of the central panel. A telephone handset with direct access to the stage manager is on the right hand side of the unit. Note the dual purpose cable/guard rail.* Photo Courtesy Theatre Projects Consultants Ltd

49 *The National Theatre, London: Olivier theatre sound control desk. The operator sits side-on to the auditorium and can therefore work extremely close to the open window. The photograph shows one of the sixteen input channel modules incorporating microphone/line sensitivity, tone controls, bass cut switch, foldback, echo send, pan (associated with groups E-F), group select, channel on/off, and PFL.*

Photo courtesy Alice (Stancoil) Ltd

1 Ring intercom speaker (SM)	**8** Talkback	**17** Output preset change-over, tape remote controls and cuelight reply button
2 PFL speaker	**9** Clear space for plot cards	
3 Monitor speakers control panel	**10** Output routing matrix preset 'X'	**18** Group faders
4 Loudspeaker circuit routing pin matrix	**11** Output routing matrix preset 'Y' with faders	**19** Group modules
		20 Channel faders
5 Group PPMs	**12** Paging and oscillator module	**21** Labelling strip
6 Auxiliary PPM and select echo, foldback etc.	**13** Labelling strip	**22** Channel modules
	14 Script space	**23** Opening window controls
7 Ring intercom speaker (technicians)	**15** Padded edge	**24** Cuelights and communications
	16 Master foldback and echo controls	**25** PPM sensitivity switch

13 Permanent sound installations

EVOLUTION

In this final chapter I should like to discuss some permanent sound installations which have been specifically designed for various new theatres in Great Britain. The post-war boom in theatre building in this country got under way during the early sixties. Not surprisingly, sound was, at the start, very much an 'also-ran'. Architects, on the whole, spent the majority of their budget on the fabric of the building, leaving a relatively small percentage for technical facilities. And it was usually decided to spend that money on stage mechanics and lighting. Lighting was then very much in vogue, with lighting designers at last being accepted as necessary rather than as a luxury. Great interest was also being aroused by the new smaller and more flexible electronic switchboards.

Nonetheless, a breed of very cost conscious sound consoles evolved, usually incorporating two tape decks with auto-stop and remote start facilities, plus two disc replay units, because tape was still not entirely trusted or understood by some of the older theatre technicians. The console might include a separate very basic microphone mixer (with over all treble and bass controls if you were lucky). The tape decks, turntable and microphone mixer with their associated gain controls would each be switchable to either or both of two output channels feeding into two power amplifiers. Loudspeakers operating via 100 volts line would be switchable to either of these amplifiers. Tone controls were minimal, sometimes only appearing as treble and bass boost and cut at the two output stages. All gain controls tended to be rotary as the range of cheap linear faders available today had yet to be introduced. Photograph 43 shows a typical example of one of the more ambitious consoles of the era. Photograph 44 shows a departure from this format in a 'desk' designed by the author in 1962 for the Old Vic theatre. It incorporates three tape decks and a six-channel microphone mixer selectable to

four output groups. Note the quadrant faders and the loudspeaker selection along the top. Another innovation was that the central control booth was actually in the auditorium. After much negotiation the theatre manager grudgingly sacrificed three seats at the back of the stalls! That is why the conditions are so cramped.

The later part of the sixties and the start of the seventies was an evolutionary period during which people became more aware of the possibilities of sound. Input channels were provided with linear faders and tone controls, and instead of operating at line level only they became switchable to microphone or line levels. This meant that the separate little microphone mixer could either be discarded altogether or kept as an extra sub-mixer for the occasional big show. Extra output channels were added to cater for stereo and the growing requirement for multiple and movable sound sources.

At this point theatre sound technicians realized that they had, by a painful process of trial and error and by striving for better standards, produced the kind of mixing desk that recording studios had evolved many years before. With this realization the technical standards of recording and broadcasting studios began to be applied to the theatre. The quality of the equipment immediately improved. This revolution occurred around 1970. The loudspeakers, their type, size, positioning and quality did not, however, improve to the same degree. And at the time of writing this is very much the problem which loudspeaker manufacturers and sound consultants are engaged upon.

Alongside these improvements in the basic sound system there also came a rationalization of the stage manager's facilities. These are, after all, mainly audio orientated, with various paging systems to dressing rooms, technicians, foyers, bars, etc., as well as the necessary cueing and intercommunication services.

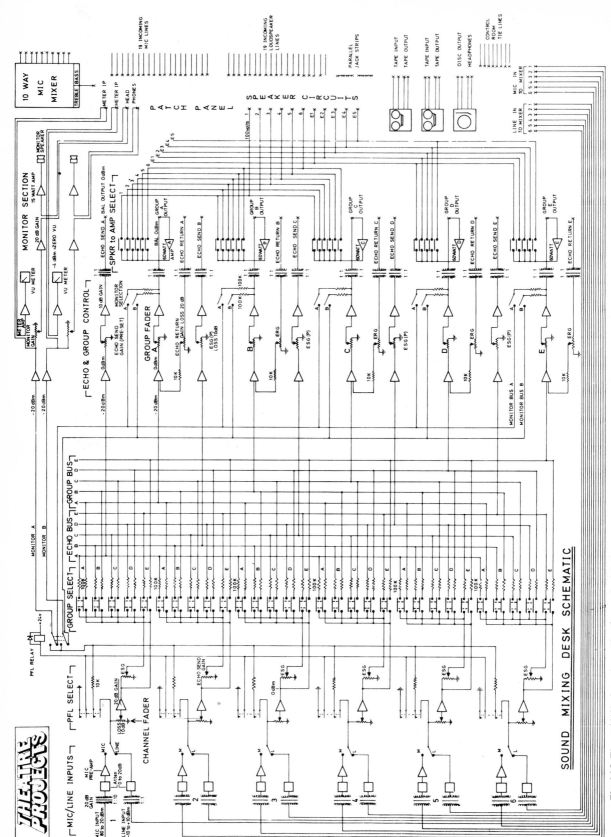

Fig 119 *Theatr Y Werin: schematic of sound mixing desk*

THEATR Y WERIN

An example of a simple yet reasonably comprehensive system is the one installed at the Theatr Y Werin, Aberystwyth in Wales (photograph 45). The budget was limited and the brief was to provide technical facilities for a small theatre which was to be used by students of the University College of Wales, local amateur groups and visiting professional companies.

SOUND RECORDING AND REPRODUCTION

The system was designed to provide reinforcement and the replay of effects in the auditorium and stage areas and facilities for the recording and make-up of effects tapes. The heart of the system is the mixing desk which is situated in a separate control room at the rear of the auditorium giving an excellent view of the stage. Microphone and loudspeaker socket outlets and permanently installed loudspeakers are all wired back to the desk; disc and tape equipment are accommodated within the control room and the whole system can be controlled at the desk. The following equipment is incorporated within the mixing console:

Two Revox tape record/replay machines. Stereo balanced line inputs and outputs appear at the jackfield (or patch panel) and the operating speeds are 15 and $7\frac{1}{2}$ i.p.s. (38 and 19 cm/s).

One disc player with tone controls and mono/stereo switch. Balanced line level outputs appear at the jackfield.

One ten-channel mono microphone mixer with master and tone controls. A balanced line level output appears on the jackfield.

The main mixer itself consists of six input channels which can each accept balanced line level or, alternatively, microphone level signals as selected at the jackfield. The insertion of a plug into a microphone input socket will automatically mute anything connected to the line input on that channel. Each input channel incorporates a fader and six individually locking push buttons for selection to any or all of the five output groups, and/or pre-fade listen.

The five output groups with faders are each tied to a 60 watt 100 volt power amplifier. Any combination of input channels may contribute to either group via the push button selection previously mentioned. The power amplifiers feed groups of loudspeakers via switching facilities. Six circuits are shared between outputs 1–3 (these are normally tied to six loudspeakers installed in the auditorium) and five more circuits are shared between outputs 4 and 5 (normally used for portable effects loudspeakers on stage). Nineteen loudspeaker socket outlets are distributed around the theatre and may be connected to these circuits via a patch in the console. Two separate monitor channels, incorporating VU meters and gain controls for the two 15 watt amplifiers driving the monitor loudspeakers, may be selected to any group. A balanced line output (0 dB) from each group appears on the jackfield to facilitate mono or stereo recording.

Nineteen microphone sockets are provided around the theatre and these are also wired back to a patch panel in the control room. Microphones can then be patched into the ten-channel microphone mixer integrated in the console and/or into the six input channels.

The installed loudspeakers consist of four line source columns for general speech reinforcement, four cabinets mounted in the auditorium ceiling containing 12 in. (300 mm) cone units for effects, and two bass cabinet and HF horn assemblies for portable use on stage.

NOTES ON OPERATING PROCEDURE

Loudspeakers, microphones and tape machines necessary for the performance are first patched into the mixing desk on the patch panels. The first tape effect is aligned on the machine so that the beginning of the magnetic tape (and the cue) is about 2 in. (50 mm) from the replay head. Then for each separate sound cue, or sequence of cues, the following procedure is carried out:

1 Loudspeaker circuits are switched on as required.

2 Input channels are routed via the group push buttons.

3 Group faders are preset to a plotted level (usually left fully open).

4 The tape machine is started by the remote push button on the mixing desk, and

5 The associated input fader is used to fade in and out the effect to predetermined levels.

When a sudden and/or critically timed effect is required (for example, a clap of thunder or a gunshot) the input channel fader may also be preset. The only operation then required is to press the tape start button at the right moment.

For more complex cues, particularly when a sound has to move (or pan) from speaker to speaker, it is more convenient to preset the input channel and work the cue on the group faders. For example, one can feed the same sound, from one input channel, out to two groups of loudspeakers; then by adjusting the group faders or the input pan fader the sound will appear to move.

At the end of each cue the tape machine will be stopped automatically by means of a translucent 'window', obtained by scraping $\frac{1}{2}$ in. (13 mm) of oxide coating off the tape with a razor blade.

Microphones can be worked as a group by balancing on the microphone mixer and then using an input channel as master. Alternatively, individual microphones can be faded up with the input channel fader preset.

Sound levels will normally be judged 'live' with the control room window open. However monitor loudspeakers have been included. These will mainly be used when recording, editing, etc.

The input channels accept a balanced 0 dB signal at 600 ohms which allows for alternative professional equipment to be used with the system. Recording outputs are at a similar level.

COMMUNICATIONS AND PERFORMANCE CONTROL

The system was designed to give all key technicians comprehensive communications during a performance or rehearsal while giving priority to the stage manager.

The stage manager's control desk is in the form of a movable control trolley which can be used in the prompt corner or in the S.M. control room at the rear of the auditorium. Communication services available to the stage manager are:

Cuelights to 14 positions
Talk-back to 5 positions
Paging to actors and staff
Ring intercom to 16 pairs of outlets

Paging to foyers and bars
Paging to the stage

Cue lights These are the standard red and green lights and are provided at all key technical areas. Each substation is provided with an 'acknowledge' button which flashes the warn light on the stage manager's control panel.

Talk-back This is to key technical areas and is initiated by the stage manager. He can address the sub-stations by selecting key switches and they are able to talk back. Although these calls are initiated by the stage manager, the sub-stations are able to call him by means of a call button which powers an indicator light on the control panel.

Ring intercom The ring intercom is a wired open speech communications ring servicing all key technical areas. At each required point it appears as two jack socket outlets, with an adjacent call light push button. Personnel using talk-back headsets may jack into one of these points to talk and listen to any other person on the ring. Pressing the call button illuminates all lights in the system and is designed to attract any technician not wearing his headset.

Paging to actors and staff Loudspeakers are positioned in all backstage areas where actors and staff might be located during a performance and the loudspeakers are fitted with volume controls which affect the show relay only. All calls from the stage manager are broadcast at a preset fixed level.

Paging to foyers and bars This enables the stage manager to make announcements ('start of performance', etc.) to the audience before they enter the auditorium. The sound control room also has use of the foyer speakers for music or recorded announcements. The stage manager has priority, so that any signal from the sound control to the foyer speakers is muted when the stage manager makes a call to this area.

Paging to stage This allows the stage manager to make loudspeaker announcements to the stage. This facility is particularly useful in rehearsals when controlling the performance from the rear of the auditorium.

The stage manager's desk is also fitted with a stop clock, extension microphone for cueing remotely from the desk, push for bar bells and a switchable white/blue working light. There are also pairs of effects keys for 6 volt and 12 volt as well as a 90 volt telephone ringing tone. The outlets for these are on the side of the desk.

THE NATIONAL THEATRE OF GREAT BRITAIN

The National Theatre of Great Britain, standing on the South Bank of the river Thames adjacent to the Festival Hall, actually houses three theatres surrounding a central dressing room block; the Upper has an adventurous open-cum-end stage format, the Lower has a more conventional proscenium style, and the studio theatre is a rectangular space with versatile seating and flexible technical facilities.

The two main theatres, although physically unalike, have almost identical stage management controls and sound mixing desk. This is to help make life a little easier for the technicians (photographs 47, 48 and 49).

PAGING

One of the biggest complications of a multi-theatre building is the possible overlap of paging to general areas both backstage and in the foyers and bars. The problem was solved by giving each stage manager an interior lit surround for each paging button which indicates when the other stage manager is using the system. If the system is occupied and he needs to make an urgent announcement he presses the button and an indicator in the other theatre starts flashing. Should the second stage manager fail to observe this signal he will lose the system automatically, after a preset number of seconds, to the other theatre.

In the general dressing room areas paging is via a single distributed loudspeaker system. Each actor can select show relay on an individual loudspeaker in his make-up cubicle. As well as show relay from three theatres there is also the possibility of switching to a fourth channel to listen to a pre-selected radio station.

Paging is provided to selected backstage areas from rehearsal rooms and the stage door. However, the stage managers have priority at all times and can cut across any other call.

CLOSED CIRCUIT TELEVISION

A CCTV camera provides a full stage picture for latecomers to watch the performance in the foyers until there is a suitable moment to enter the auditorium. The stage manager has a small television monitor built into the desk to serve as a cueing aid. Each theatre is wired for a second CCTV system for specific technical requirements, such as off-stage chorus wishing to see the conductor.

INTERCOMMUNICATION

There is a standard loudspeaking type of intercom in all the key areas where, during the day, calls may be initiated from any position. Under performance conditions, however, the stage manager has overall control and his unit becomes the master.

The free speech ring intercom system has four channels: stage manager, technical A, B and C. At the main control positions it is possible to select one of the technical channels and the stage manager. Gain controls are provided to set a balance between the two and a speak key routes the associated microphone to either channel. There are many additional points around the theatre where it is possible to connect portable headset units.

The stage manager and the production desk are able to monitor all the channels should they so wish, and the stage manager can in an emergency 'crash-call' over the lot.

Another emergency facility is the provision of telephone handsets sited at a limited number of strategic points which give direct access into the stage manager's communication channel. These can be used in the other direction by the stage manager who is able to flash an associated call light to attract anyone standing in the vicinity.

A final luxury is the possibility of switching a radio transmitter in to any of the channels. Thus roving technicians may listen to instructions via pocket radio receivers with earpieces.

SOUND SYSTEM

The mixing desks in both the main theatres are basically recording studio devices with additional output facilities to handle the complex loudspeaker routing.

Each desk has sixteen microphone/line input channels selectable to any combination of six master channels, or 'groups'. Groups E–F are selected at each channel by a single push button with an associated pan control to allow for true stereo.

There are two output presets each with twenty circuits. The upper preset has six colour coded pushes per circuit for selection to the six groups. The lower preset not only has group selection but also incorporates a fader on each circuit. A master switch changes from one preset to the other.

Sixteen of the output circuits are normally tied to sets of amplifiers driving installed loudspeakers. The other four circuits are tied to single amplifiers available for the connection of portable effects speakers. All circuits may be overplugged and rerouted at the patch panel if required.

The installed loudspeakers are as follows: stereo combinations of bass cabinets and horns mounted above the front of the stage in the Upper Theatre and around the proscenium in the Lower, four powerful bass bins and horns mounted in each auditorium ceiling (the Lower Theatre having two small supplementary units built in below the circle for the rear of the stalls), and nine sets of speakers set into the side and rear auditorium walls.

The control rooms are equipped with a selection of tape machines, a turntable, a simple reverberation unit and space for a specially designed portable sub-mixer shared between the two theatres. A generous quantity of tie lines are distributed throughout each theatre and also to a central sound/communications room. This room houses, apart from all the communications and CCTV control equipment, a studio quality reverberation unit.

The windows of the control rooms are full width and motorized so that they slide silently down into a cavity in the wall. For safety reasons as soon as the window starts to open a warning light appears on the mixing desk and all intercom and monitor loudspeakers are automatically muted.

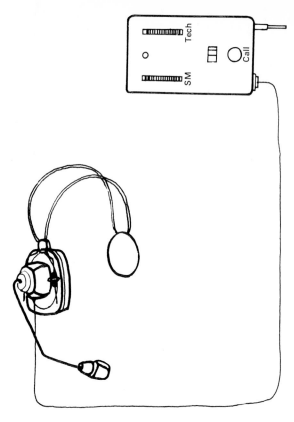

Fig 120 *National Theatre of Great Britain: ring intercom technician's portable unit.*

With such a flexible mixing desk combined with the built-in loudspeakers enveloping the audience, plus some first class stage loudspeakers the possibilities are endless. Unfortunately this manuscript is destined to be with the publishers for some months prior to the opening of the theatre, so I can only look forward with keen anticipation to seeing (and hearing) with what imagination and dexterity the system will eventually be used.

Connectors:ABTT recomendations

The Association of British Theatre Technicians published in 1974 recommendations for audio connectors for theatre sound systems. These proposals are accepted by many theatres, manufacturers and consultants and are therefore fast becoming standard in the U.K.

Loudspeaker Signals

It is recommended that loudspeaker signals should be carried in four-core cable terminating in XLR-4 connectors where pins 1 and 2 may be used for loudspeakers operating at low voltages (impedances of 3 to 16 ohms) and pins 3 and 4 are used for high voltage systems (70 or 100 volts). The wiring of the XLR-4 connector should be as follows:

Pin 1 (Red)   low voltage +
Pin 2 (Blue)   low voltage −
Pin 3 (Green)   high voltage +
Pin 4 (Yellow) high voltage −

The signal-carrying connector shall at all times be FEMALE.

Microphone and Line Level Signals

The recommendation for microphone and line level signals is that XLR-3 connectors should be employed with pin connections as follows:

Pin 1 Cable screen and circuit earth if connected
Pin 2 Positive signal + (e.g. the red of a red/black twisted pair)
Pin 3 Negative signal −

The signal carrying connector shall at all times be MALE.

Interchangeability Cross Reference of Audio Connectors

Description		Cannon	Switchcraft	Amphenol Excellite	Qwick	R.S. Components
Free Cable Connectors Pin Contacts	(3)	XLR–3–12C	A3M	91–453	91–853	X Plug 3–12C
	(4)	XLR–4–12C	A4M	91–457	91–857	X Plug 4–12C
	(5)	XLR–5–12C	A5M	91–461	—	X Plug 5–12C
	(6)	XLR–6–12C	—	—	—	—
Free Cable Connector Socket Contacts	(3)	XLR–3–11C	A3F	91–454	91–854	X Plug 3–11C
	(4)	XLR–4–11C	A4F	91–458	91–85	X Plug 4–11C
	(5)	XLR–5–11C	A5F	91–462	—	X Plug 5–11C
	(6)	XLR–6–11C	—	—	—	—
Rectangular Panel Mounts Pin Contacts	(3)	XLR–3–32	D3M	91–455	—	X Socket 3–32
	(4)	XLR–4–32	D4M	91–459	—	X Socket 4–32
	(5)	XLR–5–32	D5M	91–463	—	X Socket 5–32
	(6)	XLR–6–32	—	—	—	—
Rectangular Panel Mounts Socket Contacts	(3)	XLR–3–31	D3F	91–456	—	X Socket 3–31
	(4)	XLR–4–31	D4F	91–460	—	X Socket 4–31
	(5)	XLR–5–31	D5F	91–464	—	X Socket 5–31
	(6)	XLR–6–31	—	—	—	—
Round Panel Mount Pin Contacts	(3)	XLR–3–14	C3M	—	91–855	—
	(4)	XLR–4–14	C4M	—	91–859	—
	(5)	XLR–5–14	C5M	—	—	—
	(6)	XLR–6–14	—	—	—	—
Round Panel Mount Socket Contacts	(3)	XLR–3–13	C3F	—	91–856	—
	(4)	XLR–4–13	C4F	—	91–860	—
	(5)	XLR–5–13	C5F	—	—	—
	(6)	XLR–6–13	—	—	—	—
Round Panel Mounts (Locknut) Pin Contacts		XLR( )14N*	B( )M*	—	—	—
Round Panel Mounts Socket Contacts		XLR( )13N*	—	—	—	—
Rt. Angle Cable Connector Pin Contacts	(3)	XLR–3–16	R3M	—	—	—
	(4)	XLR–4–16	R4M	—	—	—
	(5)	XLR–5–16	R5M	—	—	—
	(6)	XLR–6–16	—	—	—	—
Rt. Angle Cable Connector Socket Contacts	(3)	XLR–3–15	R3F	—	—	—
	(4)	XLR–4–15	R4F	—	—	—
	(5)	XLR–5–15	R5F	—	—	—
	(6)	XLR–6–15	—	—	—	—

*Cannon XLR( )14N overall diameter 17/16", Switchcraft B( )M 17/64", therefore panel hole for Switchcraft smaller, otherwise they are similar.

Bibliography

Agfa-Gevaert
Tape Recording Manual
Agfa-Gevaert, London

AKG
Publications on microphones
AKG Equipment Ltd

Alkin, Glyn
*Sound with Vision: Sound
Techniques for Television and Film*
Butterworth & Co, London 1973

Allison, R. F.
*High Fidelity Systems: a User's
Guide*
Dover, New York

Altec
*Loudspeaker Enclosures: Their
Design and Use*
Altec Sound Products Division

Amos, S. W.
Principles of Transistor Circuits
Iliffe, London 1969 and Hayden
Book Co., New York

BASF
Your BASF Tape Manual
BASF

BBC
*Better Sound: BBC Radio Study
Notes*
British Broadcasting Corporation,
London 1968

Beranek, Leo L.
Music, Acoustics and Architecture
John Wiley & Sons, New York 1962

Bernstein, Julian L.
Audio Systems
John Wiley & Sons, New York 1966

Borwick, John (ed.)
Techniques of Sound Reproduction
Focal Press, London

Briggs, G. A.
Loudspeakers
Rank Wharfdale, Bradford 1958

Briggs, G. A.
Sound Reproduction
Rank Wharfdale, Bradford

**Burris-Meyer, H. and
V. Mallory**
Sound in the Theatre
Theatre Art Books, New York 1959

Common Core Series
Basic Electronics
Technical Press, Oxford 1968

Crabbe, John
Hi-Fi in the Home
Blandford Press, London 1972 and
Transatlantic Arts, New York 1972

Crowhurst, Norman H.
Audio Systems Handbook
TAB Books, Pennsylvania 1969
and Foulsham-Tab, Slough 1973

Dibdin, F. J. H.
Essentials of Sound
Macmillan Publishing, London
1968

Dolan, Robert
Music in Modern Media
Schirmer, New York 1967

Hadden, Burrell
*High-Quality Sound Production
and Reproduction*
Iliffe

**Hughes, Robert J. and
Peter Pipe**
Introduction to Electronics
English Universities Press, London
and Doubleday, New York

Jordan, E. J.
Loudspeakers
Focal Press, London 1964 and
Hastings House, New York

Judd, F. C.
Tape Recording for Everyone
Blackie & Son, Glasgow 1962

McWilliams, A. A.
Tape Recording and Reproduction
Focal Press, London 1964

Matthews, C. N. G.
Tape Recording
Museum Press, London 1968

Mee, F. G.
Sound
Heinemann, London 1967

Middleton, Robert G.
Tape Recorder Servicing Guide
Foulsham Sams & Co., Indianapolis
1970 and Foulsham-Tab, Slough

Moore, J. E.
Design for Good Acoustics
Architectural Press, London 1961

Nisbet, A.
Techniques of the Sound Studio
Focal Press, London 1963

Olson, Harry F.
Music, Physics and Engineering
Dover, New York 1966

Oughton, F.
Tape Recording & Hi-Fi
Collins, Glasgow and London 1964

**Parkin, P. H. and H. R.
Humphreys**
Acoustics, Noise and Buildings
Faber, London 1969 and Fernhill
House, New York

Rindfleisch, Dr H.
Tape Recording Technique
Agfa-Gevaert

Ritter, H.
Tape Questions and Tape Answers
BASF

Robertson, A. E.
Microphones
Iliffe, London 1973

Say, M. G. (ed.)
*Electrical Engineers' Reference
Book*
Butterworth & Co., London 1973

Scroggie, M. G.
*Foundations of Wireless and
Electronics*
Iliffe, London 1970

Sewell, E. C.
*BRE Digest 143 Sound Insulation.
Basic Principles*
HMSO, London

Sproxton, Colin
Hi Fi Yearbook
IPC Electrical-Electronic Press,
London

Warring, Ronald H.
Instructions to Radio Constructors
Museum Press, London 1966

Wood, Alexander
The Physics of Music
Methuen & Co., London and
Barnes & Noble, New York 1964

Yerges, Lyle F.
*Sound, Noise and Vibration
Control*
Van Nostrand Reinhold, New York
and London 1969

Theatrical/sound terms

English	French	Italian	German
Theatre			
theatre	théâtre	teatro	Theater
play	pièce de théâtre	lavoro teatrale	Theaterstück
opera	opéra	opera	Oper
act	acte	atto	Akt (Aufzug)
scene	scène	scena	Bild (Szene)
interval	entr'acte	intervallo	Pause
performance	représentation	rappresentazione	Vorstellung
rehearsal	répétition	prova	Probe
stage rehearsal	répétition de scène	prova di scena	Bühnenprobe
general rehearsal	répétition générale	prova generale	Hauptprobe
scene rehearsal	répétition en décors	prova dello scenario	Dekorationsprobe

Staff			
managing director	intendant	direttore del teatro	Intendant
stage director/ producer	metteur-en-scène	regista	Regisseur
director	directeur	direttore	Direktor
actor	acteur	attore	Schauspieler
opera singer	chanteur	cantante	Sänger
assistant stage manager	inspecteur	ispettore	Inspizient
ballet dancer	danseur, danseuse	ballerino, ballerina	Tänzer, Tänzerin
conductor	chef d'orchestre	direttore dell'orchestra	Kapellmeister (Dirigent)

Technicians			
technical director	directeur technique	direttore tecnico	Technischer Leiter
stage carpenter	chef-machiniste	capomacchinista	Theatermeister
stagehand	machiniste	opera o addetto alla scena	Bühnenarbeiter
chief sound man	opérateur des sons	capo di suono	Ton Meister
chief electrician	chef électricien	capo-elettricista	Beleuchtungsmeister
electrician	électricien	elettricista	Beleuchter
machinist	machiniste	macchinista	Maschinist
property man	accessoiriste	addetto agli accessori	Requisiteur
sound operator	opérateur des sons	operatore di suono	Toningenieur
stage decorator	décorateur	decoratore	Dekorateur
painter	peintre	pittore	Maler
carpenter	charpentier	carpentiere	Zimmermann

Stage			
auditorium	salle	sala	Zuschauerraum
orchestra pit	fosse d'orchestre	orchestra	Orchesterraum
stage	scène	palcoscenico	Bühne
back stage	arrière-scène	retroscena	Hinterbühne
side-stage	scène latérale	quinta	Seitenbühne
stage floor	plateau, plancher	tavolato	Bühnenboden
fly gallery	galerie d'équipes	galleria laterale	Arbeitsgalerie
grid, gridiron	cintre	soffitto del palcoscenico	Schnürboden
rolling stage	scène glissante	scena scorrevole	Schiebebühne
revolving stage	scène tournante	scena girevole	Drehbühne
under machinery	machinerie du dessous	macchinario del sottopalco	Untermaschinerie
trap	trappe	botola	Versenkung
rake	pente	pendenza	Bühnenfall
castor	roulette	rullo	Laufrolle
rostrum	praticable	praticabile	Stellage, Gerüst
step	marche	gradino	Stufe
stairs	escalier	scala	Treppe
counterweight line	équipe à contrepoids	carrucola a contrappeso	Gegengewichtszug
counterweight	contrepoids	contrappeso	Gegengewicht
rope, cord	fil	corda	Seil
wire rope, wire cable	cable	fune	Drahtseil

English	French	Italian	German
pipe	porteuse	trave centrale	Laststange
batten	perche supérieure	pertica superiore	Oberlatte
flying equipment	vol	apparecchio aereo	Flugvorrichtung
winch	treuil	argano	Winde
lift	ascenseur	ascensore	Aufzug
proscenium opening	ouverture	apertura	Bühnenöffnung
curtain	rideau	sipario	Vorhang
proscenium	avant-scène	proscenio	Proszenium
scenery	tableau, décors	scenario	Szenerie

English	French	Italian	German
Lighting			
stage lighting	éclairage de scène	illuminazione della scena	Bühnenbeleuchtung
dimmer board	commande du jeu d'orgue	quadro elettrico	Bühnenregler
dimmers, resistances	résistances	resistenze	Widerstände
floats, footlights	rampe	luce della ribalta	Rampenlichte
borderlight	herse	luce della bilance	Oberlicht
stage flood	appareils transportables	sostegni trasportabili	Versatzständer
stand, tripod, telescopic stand	pied	sostegno	Ständer, Stativ
lamp	lampe	lampada	Glühlampe
colour medium	écran de gélatine	schermo di mica	Gelatinescheibe
lens	lentille	lente	Linse
focus	foyer	fuoco	Brennpunkt

English	French	Italian	German
Sound			
acoustics	acoustique	acustica	Akustik
aerial	antenne	antenna	Antenne
alternating current	courant alternatif	corrente alternata	Wechselstrom
amp	ampère	ampere	Ampere
amplification	amplification	amplificazione	Verstärkung
amplifier	amplificateur	amplificatore	Verstärker
attenuator	attenuer (to attenuate)	attenuare (to attenuate)	vermindern (to attenuate)
bass (low frequencies)	basse	basso	bass
battery	pile	batteria	Batterie
cable	cable	cavo	Kabel
control station	jeu d'orgue	cabina di manovra	Stellwerk
direct current	courant direct	corrente continua	Gleichstrom
disc (gramophone)	disque	disco	Schallplatte
distortion	déformation	distorsione	Verzerrung
echo	écho	eco	Echo
feedback	rétro action		Rückkoppelung
frequency	fréquence	frequenza	Frequenz
fuse	fusible	fusibile	Sicherung
gain (volume)	augmentation	guaoagno	Zunahme
headset (earphone)	écouteur	cuffia	Kopfhörer
hiss	sifflement	sibilo	Gezisch
hum	ronronnement	cantarellare	Gesumme
impedance	impédance		Hindernis
intercom	intercom	intercomunicante	Sprechanlage
loudspeaker	haut-parleur	altoparlante	Lautsprecher
mains	electricité	conduttura principale	Wetz (Strom)
microphone	microphone	microfono	Mikrophon
mono	monaural	monaural	monaural
ohm	ohm	ohm	ohm
plug	fiche	spina	Stecker
radio	radio	radio	Radio
to record	enregistrer	registrare	aufnehmen
recording	enregistrement	registrazione	Aufnahme
record player	phonographe	giradisco	Plattenspieler
reverberation	répercussion	reverberazione	Widerhall
signal	signal	segnale	Signal
sockets	prises	scatole	Anschlussdosen
sound	son	suono	Ton
sound effect	bruitage		Toneffecte
splice	épisser	intrecciare	spleissen

English	French	Italian	German
spool	bobine	bobina	Spule
stereo	stereophonique	sterio	stereophonisch
switch	interrupteur	interruttore	Schalter
tape	ruban magnetique	nastro	Tonband
tape recorder	magnetophone	registratore	Tonbandgerät
tone	ton	tono	Ton
transformer	transformateur	trasformatore	Transformator
treble	soprano	sopran	sopran
voltage	voltage	voltaggio	Spannung
wattage	puissance	watt	Watt

General			
long	long	lungo	lang
short	court	corto, breve	kurz
wide	large	largo	weit
narrow	étroit	stretto	schmal
broad	large	largo	breit
large, big	grand	grande, grosso	gross
small	petit	piccolo	klein
on	sur	su	auf
up	en haut	in su, in alto	hinauf, oben
under	sous	sotto	unter
right	à droite	a destra	rechts
left	à gauche	a sinistra	links
downwards	en bas	in giú	abwärts
slow	lent	lento	langsam
fast, quickly	vite, rapide	rapido	schnell
without	sans	senza	ohne
with	avec	con	mit
low	bas	basso	niedrig
lower	plus bas	piú basso	niedriger
high	haut	alto	hoch
higher	plus haut, supérieur	piú alto, superiore	höher
too much	trop	troppo	zu viel
too little	trop peu	troppo poco	zu wenig
more	plus	piú	mehr
less	moins	meno	wenig
a third	un tiers	un terzo	ein Drittel
a quarter	un quart	un quarto	ein Viertel
good	bon	buono	gut
bad	mauvais	cattivo	schlecht
right	juste	giusto	richtig
wrong	faux	falso	falsch
repeat !	répétez !	ripetere !	wiederholen !
once	une fois	una volta	einmal
only once	une seule fois	una sola volta	nur einmal
several times	plusieurs fois	parecchi volte	mehrere Male
the last time	la dernière fois	l'ultima volta	das letzte Mal
alright, OK	en ordre, ça va	in ordine, va bene	in Ordnung
cue	signal, réplique	segno, segnale suggerimento	Zeichen, Signal, Stichwort
attention !	attention !	attenzione !	Achtung !
begin, go	en marche, on commence	si inizia	los, anfangen
stop !	halte !	alto !	halt !
take care !	attention ! prenez garde !	attenzione !	Vorsicht !
fade out	diminuer	diminuire	ausblenden
fade in	augmenter	aumentare	einblenden
music	musique	musica	Musik
up (more)	encore	piu	mehr
quiet	tranquille	quiete	ruhig
loud	fort	forte	laut
to hear	entendre	sentire	hören
to listen	écouter	ascoltare	zuhören
to hang, to clamp	suspendre	appendere	aufhangen
to mount	équiper	provvedere	ausstatten
to set up	poser	collocare	aufstellen
to earth	mettre à la terre	mettere a fersa	erden

Some useful addresses

Glossary

UK

Association of British Theatre Technicians, 9 Fitzroy Square, London W1. (Organization for collating and disseminating technical information)

Mechanical Copyright Protection Society Ltd, 380 Streatham High Road, London SW16. (For licensing the mechanical copying of a mechanically recorded work on behalf of recording companies)

Performing Rights Society Ltd, 29 Berners Street, London W1. (For licensing the public performance of a mechanically recorded work on behalf of the authors and performers)

Phonographic Performance Ltd, 62 Oxford Street, London W1. (For licensing the public performance of a mechanically recorded work on behalf of the record company)

US

This is not a complete listing of all stage sound suppliers nor does it constitute an endorsement of the equipment manufactured by these companies. For other listings, the reader should consult *Simon's Directory*, published by the Package Publicity Company, 1564 Broadway, New York, NY 10036, and the local yellow pages of the telephone directory.

AKAI America Ltd, 2139 East Del Amo, Compton, California 90220

Peter Albrecht Corp., 325 East Chicago St, Milwaukee, Wisconsin 53202

R. T. Bozak Mfg. Co., 587 Connecticut Ave., Norwalk, Connecticut

Cetec, Inc., 13035 Saticoy St, North Hollywood, California 91605

Paso Sound Products, Inc., 251 Park Avenue South, New York, NY 10010

Rauland Borg Corp., 3535 West Addison St, Dept K, Chicago, Illinois 60618

Sony/Superscope Inc., 8150 Vineland Ave., Sun Valley, California 91352

Sound 80, 2709 East 25th St, Minneapolis, Minnesota 55406

Theatre Sound, P.O. Drawer AQ, New Haven, Connecticut 06515

Triak Systems, 4225 Tuller Avenue, Culver City, California 90230

Absorption Sound conversion of acoustic energy to another form of energy within the structure of sound-absorbing materials.

Acoustical Treatment The use of acoustical absorbents, or any changes or additions to the structure to correct acoustical faults or improve the acoustical environment.

Acoustic Feedback Unwanted acoustic interaction between output and input of an audio system, usually between loudspeaker and microphone or pick-up. It can lead to continuous oscillation.

Acoustics The science of sound; including its production, transmission and effect. In popular parlance applied particularly to acoustical characteristics of halls and rooms.

Aerial Device for capturing radio signals to feed input of receiver or tuner. Also known as antenna.

Air-Borne Sound Sound transmitted through air as a medium rather than through solids or the structure of a building.

Amp Abbreviation of ampere.

Ampere Unit of electrical current flow.

Amplification, Electronic Increasing the intensity level of a sound signal by means of electrical amplification equipment.

Amplifier An electronic device for magnifying electrical signals to a level at which loudspeakers will respond.

Amplitude Magnitude, size. The maximum displacement to either side of the normal or 'rest' position of the molecules of air transmitting sound. (Also applies to any other medium transmitting sound.)

Arm Commonly, pick-up arm. Often applied to the whole pick-up assembly though strictly excludes the cartridge.

Attenuation Reducing the intensity of a sound signal.

Attenuator Device circuit for reducing signal amplitude.

Audible Capable of producing the sensations of hearing.

Baffle Structure for isolating front and rear of loudspeaker diaphragm. Sometimes applied to a loudspeaker cabinet but usually recognized as the board on which the loudspeaker is mounted.

Balance The balance of loudness between instrumental and/or vocal microphones; also between loudspeakers; also tonal balance between bass, middle and treble.

Balanced (line or circuit) System of connections in which two signal carrying conductors are equally 'live'.

Bass Low frequency end of audio spectrum below approximately 150 Hz.

Bass Reflex Type of loudspeaker cabinet with an outlet (vent or port) permitting enclosed air to be put to work to improve the efficiency at low frequencies. This is due to the inversion of phase within the enclosure so that the radiations from the port aid the radiations from the cone.

Capstan Accurate spindle which, in conjunction with pinch-wheel, drives the tape on a tape recorder.

Cardioid Microphone with 'heart-shaped' polar response, making it most sensitive in one direction.

Cartridge Tape container with continuous loop of tape (usually $\frac{1}{4}$ in.) for use in cartridge record/playback machine. Also the detachable transducer-plus-stylus part of a pick-up head.

Cassette Preloaded container with tape and spools for use on tape cassette record/playback machine. Usually with four tracks at a speed of $1\frac{7}{8}$ ips. (5 cm/s).

CCIR (International Radio Consultative Committee) Commonly refers to tape replay characteristics.

Channel Sequence of circuits or components handling one specific signal.

Chassis Metalwork on which circuit components are assembled.

Circuit An arrangement of interconnecting electrical and/or electronic components to perform some specific task. Also refers to the diagram of such an arrangement.

Coaxial Cable Type of screened cable with central conductor surrounded by an outer screen.

Cone Diaphragm of conventional moving coil loudspeaker.

Cone Surround Strip or roll of compliant material fitted to the periphery of the loudspeaker cone to seal it to the frame while permitting axial movement.

C.P.S. Cycles per second (known as Hertz).

Crossover Network Circuit for dividing the signal from an amplifier into frequency bands to feed appropriate loudspeakers ; i.e. high frequencies to the tweeter and low frequencies to the woofer, etc.

Crossover Frequency Frequency at which a crossover network divides the signal from one frequency band to another.

Crosstalk Breakthrough of signal between two supposedly separate channels. The level of wanted signal in relation to the unwanted signal is measured and expressed in decibels (dB).

Current Electrical flow measured in amperes (amps).

Cycle The repetitive pattern in any vibrating system, mechanical, electrical or acoustic. One complete cycle comprises the change of pressure, velocity, voltage or current from a zero point up to a maximum in one direction, down through zero to a minimum in the other direction, then back to zero.

Damping (of loudspeaker enclosure) Process of reducing unwanted resonant effects by applying absorbent materials to the surfaces.

Damping (of a loudspeaker) Expresses the ability of the cone to stop moving as soon as the electrical input signal ceases. Poor damping allows motion to continue briefly like an automobile with poor shock absorbers. This hangover creates a 'booming' sound in the bass frequencies masking clarity.

Damping Factor Ratio of loudspeaker impedance to amplifier source impedance. A large ratio improves the loudspeaker damping.

Decibel (dB) A standard unit representing ratios for measuring amplitude. It is used to compare two different levels : e.g. voltages, current or sound pressure levels.

Diaphragm (see Cone) Sound generating element of a loudspeaker. May be a cone driven at its apex or a metal dome driven at its periphery moving in relation to the varying sources of electrical current applied to the loudspeaker circuit.

Diffusion Dispersion of sound within a space so that there is uniform energy density throughout that space.

Din (Deutscher Industrie Normen (German industrial standards)) Commonly refers to standard plugs, sockets and tape equalization characteristics.

Dispersion The distribution of sound in a space.

Distortion Strictly, any deviation from the original in reproduction.

Drive Unit (or loudspeaker driver) The transducer unit of the loudspeaker as distinct from the enclosure or cabinet.

Drop-Out Momentary reduction or disappearance of signal on a tape recording due to inconsistent tape coating, dirt or mechanical defect.

Dual Concentric Loudspeaker Bass and treble cones or diaphragms are mounted on a common axis and separately driven via a crossover network.

Dual Cone Loudspeaker Two cones mounted on a common axis driven by a single moving coil. The inner cone, being of smaller diameter, is designed for greater efficiency at high frequencies.

Dubbing Copying of a recording by direct transfer.

Dynamic Coil (see Moving Coil).

Dynamic Range Range of signal amplitudes from highest to lowest.

Earth Loop Arrangement of interconnections between pieces of apparatus and mains earths resulting in more than one path for the earth side of a signal carrying cable.

Echo Any reflected sound which is loud enough and received late enough to be heard as distinct from the source.

Editing Process of cutting and rearranging sections of recorded tapes.

Efficiency Used in discussing the percentage of acoustic output of a loudspeaker relative to the electrical input available from the amplifier.

Enclosure (Loudspeaker) The acoustically designed cabinet or housing of a loudspeaker drive unit.

Equalization A deliberately introduced change in frequency response, e.g. tone controls, or the electrical correction for a recording characteristic.

Feedback (see Acoustic Feedback).

Flutter Rapid waver of pitch caused by fluctuations of speed in a recording. Heard as a sort of bubbly roughness.

Flutter Echo A rapid reflection pattern between parallel walls, with sufficient time between each echo to cause a listener to be aware of separate signals.

Frequency The rate of repetition in Hertz of musical pitch, as well as that of electrical signals. The number of complete cycles in one second. Low frequency refers to bass tones and high frequency to treble tones.

Frequency Response The ability of a component to reproduce a range of frequencies is called frequency response. How evenly the component responds to various frequencies within that range describes how 'flat' that response would be.

Gap Vertical slit in tape recording head, forming poles across which a magnetizing field occurs during the recording process, and into which a corresponding magnetic signal is induced during replay.

Harmonic Frequency multiple of a fundamental tone. Twice the fundamental frequency is the second harmonic, three times is the third and so on.

Harmonic Distortion A form of distortion in which unwanted harmonics are added to original signal.

Hertz (Hz) Unit of frequency equalling one cycle per second.

HF High frequency.

Howlround (see Acoustic Feedback).

Hum Unwanted low frequency tone in reproduction usually due to mains and its harmonics.

Impedance A term describing the degree to which a circuit impedes the flow of an alternating current. Measured in ohms.

Induction Production of current across a space due to electric or magnetic fields.

Infinite Baffle Loudspeaker mounting which allows no air paths between front and rear of the diaphragm.

Input Impedance Effective impedance at the input of a circuit.

Intensity The rate of sound energy transmitted in a specified direction through a given unit area.

KiloHertz (kHz) One thousand cycles per second.

LF Low frequency.

Loudspeaker Transducer system for converting electrical energy into sound energy.

Microphone Transducer for converting sound energy into electrical energy.

Mixer A device facilitating electrical mixing of a number of signals in desired proportions.

Monitoring Checking signals during a recording or the operation of a sound system by listening on a separate loudspeaker and/or by watching a level meter.

Moving Coil Type of pick-up, microphone or loudspeaker transducer in which a coil of wire moves in a magnetic field.

NAB (National Association of Broadcasters (USA)) Commonly refers to various tape standards. Also known as NARTB.

Noise Any unwanted sound.

OHM Unit of electrical resistance or impedance.

Oscillator A device for producing a continuous electrical oscillation, or pure tone, at any desired frequency.

Oscilloscope A device which provides a visual display of the wave form, frequency and amplitude of a signal.

Overloading When distortion occurs because a piece of electronic equipment is being driven beyond its signal handling capacity.

P.A. Public Address system.

Phase Refers to any part of a sound wave or an electrical signal with respect to its passage in time. Loudspeakers are in-phase when the diaphragms are oscillating in the same direction at the same time.

Pick-up Device for producing electrical signals from gramophone records.

Pitch The physical response to frequency.

Potentiometer (Pot) A variable resistor used for volume and tone controls.

Power Amplifier (see Amplifier).

Power Handling Capacity The amount of electrical power that an electronic device is capable of handling. Especially used when referring to the maximum power output of an amplifier, or the maximum power that can safely be fed to a particular loudspeaker.

Presence Quality of immediacy normally referring to microphone reproduction. Achieved by boosting the upper-middle frequencies.

Pressure Unit Moving-coil loudspeaker drive unit with a metal dome diaphragm usually used in association with a metal horn.

Resistance Amount of non-conductivity, or opposition to current flow, measured in ohms.

Resonance The tendency of any physical body to vibrate most freely at one particular frequency as a result of excitation by a sound of that particular frequency.

Reverberation The persistence of sound within a space after the source of that sound has ceased.

Reverberation Time The time in seconds required for a sound to decay to inaudibility after the sound source ceases.

Ribbon A thin corrugated strip of aluminium suspended in a magnetic field used for some microphone transducers.

Room Acoustic The natural acoustics of the listening room.

R.P.M. Revolutions per minute of a record player turntable.

Screen Metallic shield or braiding around cables to prevent electrostatic interference, especially microphone cables.

Signal-To-Noise Ratio The ratio of wanted signal to unwanted noise. Measured in decibels.

Sound Wave Sound as a disturbance which is propagated in a medium in a wave motion.

Speech Coil The metal coil in a moving coil loudspeaker.

Splice Joining together of two pieces of tape when editing.

Stylus The sapphire, diamond, etc. used in a gramophone pick-up cartridge.

Transducer Device for converting from one form of energy to another, e.g. a microphone converts from acoustic to electrical.

Unbalanced (line or circuit) System of connections in which one side of the circuit is earthed. The system employs coaxial cables.

Voice Coil The metal coil or moving coil loudspeaker.

Volt Unit of electrical force.

Watt Unit of electrical power; volts multiplied by amps.

Wattage Number of watts.

Index

Figures in italics refer to numbers of photographs